Self-Love Handbook for Women

Practical Guidance and Exercises
to Unlock Deep Self-Compassion, Practice Self-Care,
Heal from Past Wounds, and Live a Life Anchored in Love

BY LAUREN BRIM, PH.D.

"How you love yourself is how you teach others to love you."

Rupi Kaur

Table of Contents

Introduction   1

Chapter 1: Discovering Self-Love   3

Self-Love Is Our Natural State   5

Family of Origin: Who Taught You to Love Yourself?   9

Unpacking the Myth of Perfection   13

Recognizing and Halting Self-Criticism   17

Cultivating Self-Compassion   21

Chapter 2: Step-by-Step Healing For Emotional Wounds   25

Identifying Emotional Wounds from Past Relationships   26

Techniques for Emotional Detox: Letting Go of Old Hurts   30

Forgiveness of Self: A Pathway to Self-Love   35

Rebuilding Self-Worth Post-Trauma   40

Share Your Story: The Role of Vulnerability in Self-Love   45

Chapter 3: Self-Care: Daily Practices for Self-Love   49

Morning Rituals for a Self-Loving Start   50

Food Preparation and Mindful Eating   54

Mindfulness Basics for Daily Self-Love   59

Saying No to Social Media Comparison   64

Creating a Self-Love Playlist for Daily Movement   68

Connecting with Nature for Emotional Well-Being   72

Your Self-Love Language: Self-Care Tailored to You   76

Chapter 4: Healthy Boundaries and Relationships   81

Identifying Toxic and Abusive Relationships   83

Healing from Negativity in Family Dynamics   91

Setting Boundaries: A Step-by-Step Guide   96

Communication Skills for Self-Respect and Love   101

The Role of Self-Love in Romantic Relationships   107

Cultivating a Supportive Friend Network   112

Parenting with Self-Love and Compassion   116

Chapter 5: Building Inner Strength and Resilience   121

Resilience Training: Techniques for Tough Times   123

Harnessing Personal Failures for Growth and Learning   128

The Link Between Self-Love and Assertiveness   132

Handling Criticism Without Losing Self-Worth   137

Work-Life Balance and Overcoming Imposter Syndrome   143

Chapter 6: Advanced Self-Love Techniques   149

The Intersection of Spirituality and Self-Love   150

Harnessing the Power of Visualization for Self-Acceptance   154

Integrating Self-Love into Career Development   158

Financial Self-Care: Budgeting with Love   162

Community Involvement as an Expression of Self-Love   167

Chapter 7: Living a Life Anchored in Self-Love   171

Lifelong Learning as a Form of Self-Love   172

How to Love Ourselves Through Suffering or Tragedy   177

Gratitude: Celebrating Small Victories in Everyday Life   181

The Future of Self-Love: Evolving with Age and Wisdom   185

Conclusion   191

Acknowledgments   195

Recommended Reading   197

References   199

Introduction

Have you ever stood before a mirror, eyes meeting your reflection, and found it challenging to embrace the person you see? You are not alone. Many women, just like you, grapple with self-love and self-acceptance, often feeling disconnected from the love and compassion they readily offer others but withhold from themselves. But life doesn't have to be lived this way. Self-love is a way of thinking and being where you not only know you deserve the kindness, respect, and generosity inherent to love, but you give that to yourself daily. Self-love is both your natural state and a way of living and loving that was modeled for you growing up. Many have lost touch with that natural state, have never seen self-love modeled, or both.

On top of that, we experience relationships that cut us off from loving ourselves as we live through rejection, criticism, or abuse. But self-love is always there beneath the surface. Self-love and the way you love yourself can be learned or re-learned at any age. You can heal from past wounds and transform that sacred relationship with yourself to unlock deeper self-love and compassion than you ever thought possible. You can master self-love and receive all the beautiful gifts it has waiting for you.

"Self-Love Handbook for Women" was written to be a companion as you explore the realms of self-love, self-compassion, and healing the wounds from the past. This book is structured into intuitive chapters that address various dimensions of self-love—from its foundational theories to practical application in everyday life. It blends scientific research, insight from real women interviewed, and practical exercises specifically tailored for those seeking real change. Through these pages, you'll engage with content that challenges, nurtures, and inspires profound shifts in how you relate to yourself, unlocking your self-love, self-compassion, and healing. As you turn each page, I encourage you to immerse yourself deeply, reflect honestly, and embrace the exercises wholeheartedly. Your active participation is crucial to reward yourself with the profound benefits of self-love.

Discovering and nurturing self-love has been the most transformative journey of my life. It has reshaped my relationships, career, health, finances, and experience of being myself. It's a journey that never ends, but it begins with a choice to begin giving ourselves the love, self-compassion, and respect we deserve. I am confident this journey will do the same for you. Welcome to your new beginning. Let's start this beautiful self-love journey together!

Lauren Brim, Ph.D.

CHAPTER 1:

Discovering Self-Love

What is self-love? Is it our innate, natural state? Or do we learn how to love ourselves from those around us? Self-love is the most foundational yet often the most elusive quality some strive to cultivate in their lives. Someone with profound self-love likes who they are, feels good in their body, manages their life well, and gives themselves compassion when they mess up and support when they want to express themselves. Their default is to provide themselves with an abundance of loving relationships, pleasure, opportunities, and even money!

If you are still confused about self-love, think of the pure love of a new, healthy parent. Awash in this powerful love, they are compelled to give their baby attention, compassion, and empathy. They rush to meet their every need. To them, their child is the most beautiful baby they've ever seen. They treat their little bodies lovingly, shower them with gifts, and share compassion with them when they make mistakes. Self-love is loving yourself like your own baby. Self-love is parenting yourself in the way you would have loved to have been parented as a child. It is a profound acceptance and appreciation of oneself. It's a love so big that anything is possible.

Self-love is both innate and a way of being that we learn from caregivers and the world around us. Self-love is also a skill we develop, a way of caring for ourselves with actions that support our physical, psychological, and spiritual well-being. We think thoughts that are loving, respectful, and compassionate. We take actions for ourselves that are caring, considerate, and supportive. And we possess objects and relationships that reflect that level of love, such as a loving partner, healthy boundaries, and well cared-for possessions, like a beautiful home. Yet, for many, self-love does not feel innate or like something they were taught well enough by caregivers. That may be why you're here.

Self-love is a way of living and loving that can be learned at any moment when you decide to stop suffering from your self-hatred, self-rejection, or low self-worth. Have you had enough of treating yourself poorly? Maybe you love yourself, but wonder if more love is possible. Perhaps you *know* more love is possible! In this chapter, we begin to uncover ways of being that unlock your innate self-love and reverse habits that hamper self-love so that you can freely move forward on the path to loving yourself.

> **"I love myself deeply, and I'm discovering new ways of loving myself daily."**

Self-Love Is Our Natural State

Self-love is our natural state. It reflects a fundamental truth that, at our core, we are divine, infinite, lovable beings. From a spiritual perspective, each soul enters this world imbued with a divine spark, a unique expression of the universal love that permeates all existence. This inherent love forms our essence, guiding us toward self-acceptance, compassion, and inner peace. Everyone possesses this intrinsic worth and deserves to be treated with kindness and compassion. This innate sense of self-love forms the foundation for our mental, emotional, and spiritual well-being, influencing how we perceive ourselves and interact with the world.

We embody this truth effortlessly in infancy and early childhood and demonstrate a natural inclination toward self-love. Remember the joy and curiosity of your childhood? Babies and young children exhibit these qualities, along with an unapologetic self-acceptance. They express their needs and desires freely, without self-judgment or criticism. This early stage of development reflects a pure and unfiltered form of self-love, characterized by a deep connection to one's emotions and experiences. Children radiate joy, curiosity, and a profound connection with their being. They embrace their uniqueness without hesitation, embodying a pure expression of divine love untainted by external judgments or expectations. This innocence reflects our innate state of self-love, rooted in the recognition of our inherent worthiness as spiritual beings.

As we journey through life, navigating challenges and growth, our connection to this spiritual essence may become obscured by societal conditioning and the demands of the material world. External pressures, comparisons to others, and societal standards may lead us to question our worth or seek validation from external sources, forgetting the divine love that resides within us. Yet, the path to rediscovering self-love is always accessible. Spiritual practices such as meditation, prayer, and mindfulness are powerful tools that can guide us back to our true essence, empowering us to reclaim our self-worth and inner peace.

Embracing self-love from a spiritual perspective involves recognizing that we are worthy of love and compassion simply because we exist. It means honoring our spiritual journey, with its ebbs and flows, as a sacred process of growth and evolution. By reconnecting with our divine essence and treating ourselves with kindness and grace, we nurture our spiritual well-being and contribute to the collective consciousness of love and unity. Ultimately, self-love as our natural state is a spiritual awakening—recognizing the inherent divinity within ourselves and all beings. It is a journey of self-discovery and healing, one in which we embrace our authentic selves and align with the universal truth of love. Through this profound connection to our spiritual essence, we cultivate a deep sense of fulfillment, peace, and harmony in our lives and radiate this love outwards to uplift and inspire others on their spiritual paths.

"During my childhood, I felt inferior to other kids. I was socially awkward and unhappy into my early twenties. While I felt strong love for my parents and friends, I did not love myself. I started meditating at age 21 and began to become aware of myself as a spiritual being. I realized that my negative thoughts and agitated emotions were not the same as me; they were something that the real me, a spiritual being, could look at. By following a sequence of spiritual paths, I looked at these unhappy thoughts and emotions and applied my consciousness to them. It freed me from negative patterns of thought and behavior as well as agitated emotions. My self-love and love for others gradually increased over a period of 50-plus years."

Anastasia

Exercise: Loving Kindness Meditation

- Close your eyes and think of someone whom it is easy for you to love.

- Direct positive wishes of happiness, health, and well-being to that person.

- When you can successfully direct that kindness toward another, now offer some of that kindness and love to yourself.

- This practice may be difficult at first, but don't give up as it reinforces the very foundations of self-love when achieved.

Family of Origin: Who Taught You to Love Yourself?

Our family of origin plays a crucial role in shaping how we learn to love ourselves. From the earliest stages of life, our caregivers serve as mirrors, reflecting to us our emotions, needs, and worth. Their responses to our joys and sorrows teach us about validation, empathy, and self-acceptance. When our emotions are acknowledged and respected, we learn that our feelings matter, laying the foundation for self-love rooted in emotional awareness and authenticity.

The interactions within our family dynamics serve as blueprints for how we perceive and treat ourselves. Positive, nurturing interactions foster a sense of security and belonging, reinforcing the belief that we are lovable. Conversely, negative or neglectful interactions can create doubt and insecurity, impacting our self-image and ability to love ourselves unconditionally. These early experiences shape our inner dialogue and behaviors, influencing how we prioritize self-care and cultivate self-esteem.

Our family members model self-love through their actions and attitudes. When parents prioritize their own well-being, demonstrate self-compassion, and set boundaries that honor their needs, they provide a powerful example of self-love in practice. Witnessing these behaviors teaches us that self-love is not selfish but essential for personal growth and fulfillment. Conversely, if caregivers neglect their own needs or exhibit self-critical behaviors, we may internalize these patterns, potentially struggling with self-criticism and neglect in our own lives.

In essence, our family of origin serves as our first teacher of self-love, imparting lessons through both direct interactions and observed behaviors. By cultivating a supportive and loving environment, caregivers can empower their children to develop a deep sense of self-worth, resilience, and compassion. Recognizing the impact of these early influences allows us to reflect on our upbringing, identify patterns that may hinder self-love, and consciously nurture a healthier relationship with ourselves as we mature.

"When I think about self-love, I think about all the different parts of myself that I have come to know over the years. I think in my early years, I developed self-love through the eyes of my mother, who was an incredible mirror to me and accepted all of me, including my messiest and toughest thoughts, emotions, and behaviors over the course of my life, but especially in childhood. However, there are still parts of myself that I find difficult to really embrace and feel love for. This is where learning about self-compassion has been a godsend. When it feels hard to accept certain parts of myself or certain emotions that are so difficult to tolerate or even admit, like shame, learning to meet those parts of me with compassion has been an easier way in. It helps me treat myself in a loving way even if I don't necessarily feel the love for myself. That has brought me so much peace in some of my hardest moments and then the door is opened for me to access acceptance of myself as my mom modeled for me so early on. I imagine that I will continue to learn many more things about myself in this lifetime, so the journey of working on self-love will continue."

Gia

Exercise: Be with Yourself in the Mirror

- Stand in front of a full-length mirror— if you have one; if not, any mirror will do—and take in your whole body. If you are feeling courageous, do this naked.

- Start with the top of your head and make your way down to your feet, giving your attention to every part of you and describing to yourself, out loud if you like, what you see.

- Then, find at least one part of your body you like and say out loud what you like about that part. Find another if you can.

- Finally, contact your eyes in the mirror and give yourself unconditional love. You can say out loud, "I love you, [your name]." Tell yourself things that you love about yourself.

- If there are parts of your body you feel like sharing a loving touch or some loving words with, do that as well.

Unpacking the Myth of Perfection

Our world is inundated with ideals of perfection at every turn—from billboard ads showcasing flawless skin to social media feeds celebrating unattainable lifestyles. These images permeate our consciousness, setting a bar for perfection that is not just unrealistic but fundamentally unachievable. We live in a society that equates worth with perfection, and we have media portrayals that showcase success without struggle. Multiple studies[1] have found a strong link between prolonged social media use and an increased risk for depression, anxiety, loneliness, and self-harm. Why is that? When we buy into the myth of perfection, we compare ourselves to others, degrading our worth and accomplishments.

The concept of beauty is also heavily impacted by the myth of perfection. Although what is considered beautiful changes from generation to generation, the impact of these ever-changing standards on women has been profound. Beauty ideals often become increasingly specific and unattainable as they evolve, creating a mass market for beauty products, treatments, or even surgeries that promise to help women meet these unrealistic expectations. This continual push toward a singular beauty ideal can lead to a host of negative outcomes, including poor body image, eating disorders, and diminished self-esteem. The pressure to conform to these standards can make appreciating your unique beauty and worth challenging – if you're constantly measuring yourself against an unachievable ideal.

Pursuing the myth of perfection manifests as a continuous loop of self-evaluation and critical comparison, where your achievements, like

---

1   Azem L, Al Alwani R, Lucas A, Alsaadi B, Njihia G, Bibi B, Alzubaidi M, Househ M. Social Media Use and Depression in Adolescents: A Scoping Review. Behav Sci (Basel). 2023 Jun 6;13(6):475. doi: 10.3390/bs13060475. PMID: 37366727; PMCID: PMC10294999.

being great at your job, getting your kids to school on time, or putting together a nice outfit that complements your figure, are overshadowed by a chronic sense of insufficiency. This striving for an unattainable ideal leads to dissatisfaction and a nagging feeling of failure, which can spiral into more severe emotional distress, self-criticism, and even self-hatred. So how do we love ourselves and shift from pursuing the perfection myth to focusing on personal growth, self-acceptance, and honoring our individual, innate beauty?

Unpacking the myth of perfection starts with redefining what excellence and beauty mean to you. Start by identifying traits or characteristics you appreciate about yourself that may not align with conventional standards. It may be the strength of your body, the power of your empathy, the curve of your smile, how you show up as a friend or the resilience of your spirit. Recognizing and valuing these unique attributes can shift your focus from striving to meet external standards to celebrating your individuality. You can consciously create kind, achievable standards that align with your capabilities and aspirations. Recognize that each step forward is a victory worth celebrating, no matter how small. By altering your perspective this way, you liberate yourself from the chains of perfectionism and open the door to more self-love!

"I used to tie my self-worth and self-love to my physical appearance. I was obsessed with how I looked and assumed others found value in me based on the same things I did. Then a year ago I gave birth to two beautiful twin girls, and I never looked worse on the outside. I struggled for months with being overweight and having such tired, old-looking skin. In time, though, I just fell in love with motherhood. My weight didn't really change too much, but the way I embraced my role and put myself aside for my babies gave me a much deeper sense of self-acceptance than I ever had. Then eventually the weight came off easier as a result of my inner self-love."

Sam

Exercise: Redefining Beauty

- Take a moment to write down the qualities or features you most admire in yourself and others that are often not recognized by mainstream beauty standards.

- Next to each trait, write a brief note about why it is valuable or important. This exercise can help shift your perspective and affirm that beauty is a multifaceted and deeply personal concept.

Recognizing and Halting Self-Criticism

Self-criticism is a common habit that many of us indulge in without fully recognizing its profound impact on our mental health and overall well-being. Perhaps you find yourself replaying a small mistake in your mind repeatedly. Or you catch yourself using harsh words with yourself when you fail to meet your expectations. These self-criticism patterns often stem from various triggers, including comments from others that we internalize over time, past failures (real or perceived), and societal pressures to perform or conform. It is essential to understand these triggers and the self-critical thoughts they evoke to begin the process of silencing the inner critic.

The first step toward changing how we treat ourselves is to recognize these negative thought patterns. This process involves becoming an observer of your own mind, noticing when self-criticism arises without immediately reacting to it. For instance, if you're preparing a presentation and think, "I'm not good at this. I'm going to embarrass myself," recognize this as a moment of self-criticism (your "inner critic"). It can be helpful to maintain a daily journal where you document instances of self-critical thoughts, what triggered them, and how they made you feel. This practice not only aids in recognizing patterns, but also in understanding the contexts that exacerbate self-criticism.

Once you have identified these thoughts, the next step is interrupting them. One effective technique is the Stop Technique—a method where you mentally or verbally say "Stop" when you catch yourself engaging in negative self-talk. This acts as a brake on the spiraling negative thoughts and provides a pause where you can redirect your thinking. Following the "Stop," engage in a constructive or neutral activity to shift your focus. This could be breathing deeply, stretching, or reciting a positive affirmation. The key is to disengage from the self-critical thought and replace it with an action that soothes or distracts you.

Replacing negative self-talk with positive affirmations or compassionate self-dialogue is a powerful way to alter habitual thinking patterns. Start by creating a list of affirmations or self-compassionate statements that resonate with you and reflect the qualities you wish to embody or recognize in yourself. These might include statements like, "I am doing my best, and that is enough," or "I am learning and growing every day." Repeat these affirmations during times when you would typically engage in self-criticism. Over time, this practice helps lay down new neural pathways, leading to a more supportive and compassionate internal dialogue.

This shift from self-criticism to self-support is not only about stopping negative thoughts, but also about actively cultivating a kinder, more forgiving inner voice. It's a transformation that, while requiring patience and practice, is incredibly rewarding. As you become more adept at recognizing, interrupting, and replacing self-critical thoughts with affirming and compassionate responses, you'll find that your self-esteem, overall resilience, and emotional well-being improve as well. Engaging in these practices daily sets a foundation for a more positive and affirming relationship with yourself, which is the essence of true self-love.

"I think when I started loving myself more in my twenties, I noticed that I just said kinder things to myself than when I was a teenager or kid. I can still be critical of myself in my head, but I'm more aware of the shift to a critical voice now. And it's like I have an option to stop doing it, rather than just believing that voice is the truth and that I should listen to it. I can get out of that critical place faster now."

Kylie

Exercise: Shifting from Self-Criticism to Self-Support

- Take five minutes to reflect on some typical phrases you use to criticize yourself.

- Write them down and then cross them out and replace them with a phrase of self-support.

- Consider how this new standard of interrupting self-criticism could reduce self-harm and improve how you feel about yourself. This exercise is about learning new ways of cultivating self-love through loving, supportive, and compassionate ways of speaking to yourself.

Cultivating Self-Compassion

Self-compassion involves treating oneself with kindness, concern, and support when confronted with suffering. While not always easy or familiar, the benefits of practicing self-compassion are grounded in rigorous psychological research and are worth understanding. Self-compassion is strongly associated with psychological well-being and increased feelings of happiness, optimism, and curiosity about life. Self-compassionate people can admit mistakes, modify behavior that doesn't serve them, and show more initiative to make needed changes and take on new challenges. Practicing self-compassion increases feelings of safety, trust, and connectedness. The ability to practice self-compassion is a core component of self-love.

Several studies[2] have provided empirical support for the benefits of self-compassion over self-criticism. They found that participants who engaged in a self-compassion exercise had lower cortisol levels and reported greater emotional resilience than those who did not. Chronic activation of cortisol can lead to serious health problems, including heart disease, diabetes, and a compromised immune system. Additionally, self-compassion researcher Dr. Kristin Neff revealed that self-compassion was strongly associated with emotional well-being, suggesting that individuals who were kinder to themselves faced life's challenges with more grace and less anxiety. There are physical and mental health benefits to treating ourselves lovingly and compassionately. Self-compassion shields us from the negative effects of stress.

---

2   Neff KD. The Role of Self-Compassion in Development: A Healthier Way to Relate to Oneself. Hum Dev. 2009 Jun;52(4):211-214. doi: 10.1159/000215071. PMID: 22479080; PMCID: PMC2790748.

Dr. Neff, a pioneer in the field of self-compassion defines it as compassion turned inward. She breaks it down into three components: self-kindness, common humanity, and mindfulness. Self-kindness is how we are caring and understanding with ourselves rather than being cold, judgmental, or mean. The common humanity component is how we recognize that suffering and personal inadequacy are part of the shared human experience—something we all go through rather than something that we experience alone. Lastly, mindfulness, in relation to self-compassion, is how we bring awareness to the critical thoughts and emotions that arise, making us less likely to be overwhelmed by them and more able to choose more compassionate and loving thoughts in their place.

Incorporating self-compassion into your daily life can profoundly impact your self-love journey and your emotional and physical health. You can foster a healthier, more resilient self by learning to respond to personal failings and painful situations with kindness and understanding rather than harsh judgment. Acknowledging the feelings that arise, meeting them with gentleness, and choosing to be kind to yourself in your perceived failures is how you put self-love into action. Through the lens of science, self-compassion emerges not just as a beneficial practice but as a vital component of overall well-being, offering a powerful antidote to self-criticism and a pathway to practices that embody and encourage self-love.

"My whole family turned against me when my father was dying, and I had to really find that love for myself and believe in myself during that experience. Being able to have self-compassion for myself at that moment led me to have self-compassion for them. It was one of the biggest lessons of my life. In grief, people will do the darndest things. But how you relate to the issue is the issue. I was like "Victim, victim, victim," but my father is dying, and it makes sense he's chosen two other people over me, given our history. How do I love myself and accept myself during this crisis? How do I keep moving past judgment? So, I finally accepted it instead of fighting it. That was the most loving thing I could do for myself. This is happening. It's not going to stop. So how was I going to be with myself? I don't have to be perfect in this crisis. I had to practice a lot of self-love and self-forgiveness to get through it."

Danielle

Exercise: Mindfulness for Self-Compassion

- Take a few minutes each day to integrate a mindfulness meditation focused on self-compassion into your day.

- Begin by finding a quiet space where you can sit comfortably without interruptions.

- Close your eyes and focus on your breath. As you settle into awareness, consider a situation that's causing you stress or pain. Observe the feelings that arise, acknowledging them without judgment.

- Now, send yourself messages of kindness and support as you would to a friend. For instance, you might silently say, "It's okay to feel this way," or "I am here for you," or give yourself a loving touch, like a hug or gentle, loving strokes to your forehead or cheek. It's crucial to genuinely feel the compassion directed toward yourself, allowing it to soothe you.

Step-by-Step Healing For Emotional Wounds

What wounds are you still carrying? Emotional wounds from our past can hold us back in ways we barely recognize. They linger beneath the surface of our daily interactions and emotional responses, subtly influencing our behavior and shaping our current relationships. Have you ever wondered why specific actions or words trigger an unexpected emotional response? Or a spiral of self-criticism? These reactions stem from emotional wounds left by past relationships. But the good news about a wound is that it can heal. And many find that the scar left behind when it heals only adds to its beauty. This chapter will guide you through identifying, understanding, and ultimately healing the emotional wounds affecting your relationship with yourself and others, thus freeing you to unlock more self-love and engage more fully and healthily in your present and future relationships.

"I love myself for staying open to love, even if I've been hurt in the past."

Identifying Emotional Wounds from Past Relationships

The first step in healing is to recognize the source of your wounds. Reflect on your past relationships—familial, romantic partnerships, or even friendships. Try to identify specific instances or patterns that might have left emotional wounds. These moments will hold a lot of pain and won't feel resolved. It could be a criticism, a betrayal, a painful breakup, or emotional neglect. In those memories of pain, ask yourself: *What did I believe or decide to be true about myself in that moment?* Because while it might feel like the hurt you carry is because of what someone did to you, it's the impact it made on your relationship with yourself where the deeper emotional wound lies.

For example, perhaps your parents were always working, and you felt abandoned and neglected. When you close your eyes and return to that moment, what was the thought inside your head? "They don't love me," "I'm not good enough," or "I am always alone"? These experiences with the outside world affect your relationship with yourself because of *the decisions you make about yourself at that moment*: I'm not lovable, I'm not good enough, I'll never have what I want, etc. Each relationship might harbor different wounds, or some might repeat and reinforce the earlier ones. Knowing what you decided to be true about yourself in those moments is essential to healing your emotional wounds.

These emotional wounds influence our relationship with ourselves and our behavior in ways we might not readily see. For instance, if you've been criticized frequently in a past relationship, you might do the same to yourself without realizing it. Therefore, you are overly sensitive to anything you perceive as criticism from others, even if it's just feedback, perceiving it as criticism even when it's not intended. Or if someone abruptly broke up with you, and you had the thought,

"Everyone always leaves me," or "I can't make a relationship work," you may unconsciously do things to recreate breakups, like pushing the other person away. Our wounds affect how we see ourselves, which affects our behavior, and our behavior creates the life we live.

Acknowledging the stories we believe about ourselves is crucial in the healing process. Recognizing and accepting that you have these wounds is the first step toward recovery. It's akin to treating a physical wound: Cleaning and caring for it can promote healing. Similarly, acknowledging emotional wounds allows you to start addressing them constructively. This acknowledgment also helps prevent the repetition of harmful patterns. Being aware of how past hurts may be influencing your self-talk and behavior allows you to make different choices in the future, choices that are healthier for you and your current relationships.

Exploring and acknowledging past emotional wounds can be painful, and many people would prefer to numb out with food, alcohol, sex, or Netflix. But you're here to grow your self-love! Healing is hard work and requires courage and honesty, but it will lead to greater self-understanding, emotional freedom, and self-love. As you work through these steps, remember to be as compassionate and patient with yourself as you would be with a dear friend. Healing is a lifelong journey, and taking your time to work through these experiences is okay. No matter how small, each step forward is a step toward a healthier, more loving relationship with you.

"I was in a really unhealthy relationship for a long time thinking there was something wrong with me. But as soon as I got out of that relationship and did some healing, I realized there was nothing wrong with me! That was just a story I kept repeating to myself when I was with him."

Brittany

Exercise: Healing Relationship Wounds (2 parts)

- Part 1: Start by writing or meditating on a past relationship that holds some emotional wounds. Describe the relationship and note any particular incidents that hurt you. Reflect on how you reacted then and how you might be reacting to similar situations now. What did you tell yourself in this experience? What did you decide about yourself?

- Then ask yourself: Is what I decided about myself true? This exercise can help you see how past pain influences your current emotional responses and question your decisions that are still with you today.

- Part 2: Now, visualize the person or situation that caused you pain. In your mind's eye, go back to that moment and allow yourself to express the feelings you might have held back. Then, slowly envision offering forgiveness to the person—not for their sake, but for your healing. This doesn't mean forgetting or excusing what happened but instead allowing yourself to let go of this pain's hold on your present life.

- Then extend that same forgiveness to yourself.

- Repeat until you've revisited the painful memories you've identified.

Techniques for Emotional Detox: Letting Go of Old Hurts

Emotional detoxification refers to a conscious effort to release and clear out accumulated negative emotions that might be impacting your mental and physical health. This process is vital for anyone seeking to overcome the residual effects of past hurts, which, if left unaddressed, can manifest as persistent sadness, anxiety, or anger. By purging these toxic emotions, you pave the way for renewed emotional resilience, a healthier body, and a more positive outlook on life. There are many ways to detox emotionally, and a great deal of research supports these methods, so let's review some of them below.

Grounding techniques are designed to bring you back to the present moment, diverting your attention away from distressing memories or worries about the future. A simple yet effective grounding method is deep breathing while feeling the earth beneath you and the total weight of your body in space. Start by finding a quiet place where you can sit comfortably without interruptions. If you can remove your shoes and put your feet on the grass or dirt, that's even better! Close your eyes and take a slow, deep breath through your nose, allowing your stomach to expand fully. Hold this breath for a few seconds, then exhale slowly through your nose or mouth while sending your awareness down through your body and into the earth. Repeat this process several times, focusing fully on each breath and how you feel in your body, and with the awareness of sending your energy down into the earth, like a tree's roots. This helps reduce the immediate physical symptoms of stress, such as elevated heart rate and aids in centering your mind, making it easier to approach painful emotions or memories with calm and control.

Mindfulness meditation is another powerful grounding technique for letting go of painful emotions. Sit quietly and paying attention to your thoughts, sounds, sensations, or body parts, bringing your attention back whenever your mind wanders. You can do this practice at any time of day and in any location, with your eyes open or shut. Regular mindfulness helps cultivate awareness and presence, which is incredibly beneficial when dealing with emotional surges during the detox process.

Creative arts therapies, such as painting, music, or dance, offer another avenue for emotional release. These activities allow you to express your feelings nonverbally, which can be particularly useful if you struggle to articulate them or if they are too overwhelming. All the pain, fear, sadness, or anger can find their way onto the page, canvas, or simply out into the ethers as you paint, dance, or play them out. Engaging in creative activities can also boost your mood and self-esteem, reinforcing positive feelings and reducing the impact of negative ones.

Exercise and sweating are an effective method to detox emotions. Exercise improves blood circulation, increases our breath cycle, and moves our lymphatic fluid, clearing out stagnant emotions in our tissues. Running, punching, stretching, and dancing can all help us move through more difficult emotions to access, like anger or helplessness. Many people find healing from regularly sitting in saunas, a practice that dates back thousands of years in Native American cultures. Just make sure you practice this safely. Don't overdo it, and be sure to replace the salt, potassium, and minerals you lose when you sweat through food or supplements.

Expressive writing is a highly therapeutic tool for emotional detox. It involves writing down your thoughts and feelings about distressing experiences as they come without worrying about grammar or style. This exercise helps process those emotions by putting them into words, often providing a new perspective and relief. Set aside a few minutes each day to write freely. Over time, you may notice patterns in your thoughts and feelings that provide deeper insights into what triggers your emotional responses.

Creating a supportive environment is crucial for a successful emotional detox. This means both a physical space where you feel safe and comfortable and an emotional space where you feel supported and understood. Physically, it might involve arranging a peaceful corner in your home where you can meditate, write, or engage in creative activities without disturbance. Emotionally, it means surrounding yourself with people who understand and support your healing process. This could be friends, family, or a support group where members share similar experiences and can offer empathy and encouragement. Remember, healing is not a solitary journey; having a supportive network can make a significant difference in your ability to manage and move beyond past hurts.

By incorporating these techniques into your routine, you actively participate in your emotional healing. Each method offers a unique way to confront and clear emotions that are negatively affecting you, helping you reinstate a sense of peace and balance in your life. As you continue to practice these techniques, you may not only feel lighter and healthier, but also become better at managing emotional surges and more adept at recognizing and nurturing your emotional needs. This proactive approach to emotional health is vital to living a life of self-love and enjoying healthy relationships.

"My self-love really expanded when I moved into a home space, all by myself, without my housemates! It was 2018; at the time, I was 32 years old and had been teaching yoga for a few years. I now understand why my heart opened so wide; I was able to be selfish, and I didn't have to consider anyone else in this safe, sacred space. It was all mine, and I wasn't distracted by others' thoughts, emotions, or external energy. I really had the opportunity to focus on the qualities that I loved, such as gratitude, spirituality, and nutrition, to find out who I am as a human being on this earth."

Laura

Exercise: Emotional Detox—Give the Emotion a Color

- To detox stubborn emotions from the body, identify the emotion you are feeling: sadness, anger, fear, worry, grief, or disgust (any variation on any of these is okay; for example, anger could be rage, annoyance, or impatience; Google the emotion color wheel if you need help).

- Then, with your eyes closed, scan your body to see where you feel that emotion sitting in your body (for example, the face, pelvis, arms, and genitals). When you see or sense it, give it a color and, if you like, a texture. (Example: I see purple in my throat or black in my belly).

- Lastly, put your hands over that area and see all the color moving out of that region of your body and into your hands, which you slowly move away from your body. Visualize the emotion being transported from your hands down into the earth, where Mother Nature can break it down.

- Keep going back to the area until you don't see any more emotion sitting in the tissue.

Forgiveness of Self: A Pathway to Self-Love

After an emotional wound has surfaced for healing and the emotion has been released, we are sometimes left with the weight of responsibility for our choices. This weight can feel like more than we can bear. After all, we chose those partners, told ourselves those stories, and didn't protect or treat ourselves as our loved and precious child. Or perhaps the pain of what others have done to us still weighs heavily on our hearts and bodies. We've said what we can say and expressed our pain, but we still can't shake that final weight of grief and anger. This is where self-forgiveness comes in.

Forgiveness is a concept often misunderstood and conflated with the idea of reconciliation. However, true forgiveness is the personal process of letting go of deep-seated resentment and anger toward ourselves or those who have wronged us. The purpose of self-forgiveness is not to excuse harmful actions but rather to liberate oneself from the toxic burden of grief, anger, and judgment, which can hinder our growth and emotional well-being. Think of forgiveness as a choice: By choosing to forgive yourself, you decide to share compassion and love with yourself. Forgiveness of others, or sharing compassion and love with them, naturally extends from our forgiveness of self.

A powerful two-part forgiveness practice from the Spiritual Psychology program at the University of Santa Monica, recognizes that an inability to forgive ourselves is rooted in our self-judgment. Identifying where we are judging ourselves can help release the judgment that is hindering self-forgiveness and, ultimately, self-love:

1. Close your eyes and put your awareness on where you are having difficulty forgiving yourself. When you can see it, fill in

the following phrase: "I forgive myself for judging myself *as* [fill in the blank with the self-judgment]."

Phrases might sound like "I forgive myself for judging myself as a bad sister," "I forgive myself for judging myself as a loser," or "I forgive myself for judging myself as a failure to my children." You are not forgiving yourself for your actions or inaction from the past, but for the judgment you have about yourself from that experience. Repeat the phrase over and over until the phrase starts to feel authentic or you feel lighter.

2. The second part of this exercise is just as important. It follows up on the first phrase by filling in the following: "Because the truth is [fill in the blank with what is true about you]."

Phrases might sound like "Because the truth is I have been a good sister," "Because the truth is I am a wonderful, hard worker," or "Because the truth is I go above and beyond for my children every day." Get ready because this practice will bring up some powerful feelings of self-love as you forgive yourself for judging yourself and identify the truth!

Studies[3] have shown that forgiveness can significantly improve health, including reduced anxiety, lower blood pressure, and improved heart health. Forgiveness helps us let go of resentment, enhancing our capacity for kindness, empathy, and love toward ourselves and others. This shift can dramatically alter our lives, opening new choices and healthier relationships. It fosters a greater sense of inner peace and stability, allowing us to engage more fully with life without the weight of past hurts holding us back.

---

3   Toussaint LL, Shields GS, Slavich GM. Forgiveness, Stress, and Health: a 5-Week Dynamic Parallel Process Study. Ann Behav Med. 2016 Oct;50(5):727-735. doi: 10.1007/s12160-016-9796-6. PMID: 27068160; PMCID: PMC5055412.

Self-forgiveness is a deeply personal act that can unlock doors to emotional healing and self-love that might have seemed forever closed. It is also a journey that doesn't always happen overnight. Keep revisiting this practice of forgiving yourself for your actions and your judgment of yourself for those actions. Take responsibility for both and move forward. Self-forgiveness is about making peace with your past. It's a gift to oneself—a way to reclaim your energy, peace, and joy.

"Every time I forgive myself for judging myself as bad, I step into greater union with myself. It bridges the divide within myself and makes me whole."

Ahna

Exercise: Self-Forgiveness

- Find something you are still angry, sad, or ashamed about from your past or present situation.

- Then, identify how you have judged yourself in that situation. Place one hand on your heart and the other on your belly and say aloud, "I forgive myself for judging myself as [fill in the blank]. Repeat it as many times as you need to until you feel lighter.

- The second and most important part of this exercise is to recognize what is true about yourself in that scenario. Take a moment to reflect on this and say "Because the truth is I [fill in the blank]."

- Repeat this exercise until you feel profound peace and an increase in self-love.

Rebuilding Self-Worth Post-Trauma

Trauma can profoundly impact your self-worth, often leaving you feeling powerless, vulnerable, and unworthy. These feelings are not reflections of your true self but rather shadows cast by your traumatic experiences. Trauma is defined, diagnosed and treated with specific criteria by licensed psychologists, but it is loosely defined by others as a lasting emotional response to a stressful, frightening, or distressing event that is difficult to cope with or out of one's control. Most of us have experienced something that falls under this definition, and some of us have experienced more trauma than others could ever imagine. A traumatic experience might be happening to you as you read this book. Understanding how these experiences have shaped your perception of self-worth is crucial to restoring a loving relationship with yourself.

Traumatic experiences often lead to negative self-perceptions. Blaming yourself is one of the ways you can feel some control when the actions of others or the experiences of life remove your sense of control. This is why we see children blame themselves when they don't receive what they need from a parent. It is less painful to think negatively about themselves and blame themselves for their parent's shortcomings than to feel they have no control over whether their parent loves and cares for them. This sustained experience of self-blame turns into a diminished sense of self-worth, where you might feel less deserving of happiness, success, or love throughout your life. Such feelings are intensified if the trauma involves betrayal or violation from those you trusted, as these experiences can lead to more profound questions about one's value and judgment. It's essential to address these feelings not as truths about your character but as emotional responses to your experiences. Recognizing this distinction is the first step toward healing.

Building resilience is critical to restoring self-worth post-trauma. Resilience development involves strategies that strengthen your ability to cope with stress and recover from adversity. One effective resilience-building method is to engage in writing exercises that focus on identifying and nurturing your strengths. Write about a time you overcame a challenge or begin the practice of keeping a gratitude journal where you regularly jot down things you are grateful for. These exercises reinforce your capability and resourcefulness, which are vital for rebuilding self-esteem. Engaging in empowering activities is another decisive step in this process. Activities that reinforce your competence and autonomy help rebuild your confidence and assert your independence. Taking up new hobbies or learning new and challenging skills provides a sense of accomplishment. Volunteering is another avenue for rebuilding self-worth, as it affirms your ability to contribute positively to society and connects you with others, helping reduce feelings of isolation that often accompany trauma.

Working with a therapist or coach who specializes in trauma is a necessity for many, and there are many effective techniques for helping one move past the effects of trauma on the body-mind. Cognitive Processing Therapy for Post-Traumatic Stress Disorder (PTSD), Eye Movement Desensitization and Reprocessing (EMDR), Somatic Therapy, BodyTalk, Yoga for Sexual Trauma, and Emotional Freedom Technique (also known as tapping) are powerful tools designed to alleviate emotional distress and foster deep-seated self-love. These innovative methods combine modern psychology research with elements of traditional body-mind medicine to provide relief from stress, anxiety, and a host of other emotional issues. Studies[4] have shown that tapping can significantly decrease symptoms of depression,

---

4   Bach D, Groesbeck G, Stapleton P, Sims R, Blickheuser K, Church D. Clinical EFT (Emotional Freedom Techniques) Improves Multiple Physiological Markers of Health. J Evid Based Integr Med. 2019 Jan-Dec;24:2515690X18823691. doi: 10.1177/2515690X18823691. PMID: 30777453; PMCID: PMC6381429.

anxiety, and PTSD. One theory behind its effectiveness is that tapping on meridian points while focusing on negative emotions sends signals to the brain's amygdala, which helps reduce distressing feelings, facilitating emotional freedom where self-love can flourish.

Lastly, a regular practice of self-affirmations, or mantras, can profoundly influence your self-perception and aid in healing from trauma. Affirmations are positive statements that, when repeated often, can help you internalize feelings of worthiness and resilience. Start by choosing affirmations that resonate with your desired state of being, such as "I am worthy of love and respect" or "I am capable of overcoming challenges." Repeat these affirmations daily, preferably in front of a mirror, to reinforce their positive messages and gradually replace the negative narratives shaped by trauma. To remind yourself to use your affirmations, write them on paper and tape them onto the mirror where you get ready or some other place where you can see them regularly. Listening to affirmation recordings in the car or while getting ready for bed are also excellent practices.

These strategies for rebuilding self-worth after trauma are not just about recovering what was lost but about fostering a renewed, more robust sense of self, capable of facing future challenges with confidence and grace. By recognizing the impact of trauma, engaging in resilience-building activities, seeking out therapy, participating in empowering tasks, and practicing affirmations, you'll nurture a resilient and positive self-image. This renewed self-worth will empower you to move forward, not defined by your past but inspired by your capacity for recovery and growth.

"When I think about something painful from the past now, I just repeat to myself: 'I am loved, and I am at peace.' That really calms me down and puts a smile on my face. When I say it, I believe it."

Latoya

Exercise: Write Your Personal Affirmations

- Create ten personal affirmations that make you feel better about yourself or your goals. These statements should be positive, concise, and in the present tense as if they are already true. For example, "I am confident in my ability to succeed," "I am beautiful," or "I embrace each moment with peace and joy." They should feel powerful and pertinent to you.

- Repeat them out loud with conviction until you feel a strong emotional response. This can shift your mindset from doubt and fear to confidence and strength. By consistently affirming your positive qualities or goals, you'll reinforce your ability to rise above these challenges, embedding these affirmations deeply into your subconscious.

- Now, sit in quiet reflection and repeat your affirmations slowly, allowing each word to sink deeply into your consciousness. By affirming your worth and capabilities regularly, you'll create an empowering dialogue with yourself, one that supports your growth and transformation.

Share Your Story: The Role of Vulnerability in Self-Love

In her now-famous TED Talk on vulnerability, researcher Brené Brown shares that while many people live in fear of what others will think of them, we have to live vulnerably to experience everything we are longing for in this life, including love, joy, and belonging. She found that while shame unravels connection, those with the courage to be imperfect, to share authentically, and to let themselves be seen are more likely to feel worthy of love and belonging. Vulnerability, often misconceived as a weakness, is a profound strength, particularly in self-love. It involves the courage to show your true self to others and open up about your feelings, desires, and fears without the façade of perfection often demanded by social norms. In self-love, vulnerability signifies the acceptance of one's true nature, with all its imperfections, weaknesses, and strengths, which is a fundamental component of genuine self-love.

The benefits of vulnerability are manifold. When you stop hiding your true self, you live more genuinely. This authenticity attracts deeper connections with others, as people are drawn to honesty and openness. Relationships founded on vulnerability are more robust, exciting, and more fulfilling. Vulnerability leads to increased self-acceptance. Recognizing and expressing your true feelings helps you understand yourself better and accept your emotions as valid. As a trusted friend, skilled therapist, or even a stranger validates what you've been through and maybe shares their story with you, a shared humanity unfolds, creating connection, belonging, and safety to be ourselves. Share something true about yourself that you usually keep hidden, perhaps an insecurity or a dream you fear is too big. Over time, as trust deepens, you may share more significant vulnerabilities, leading to even deeper relationships and self-understanding.

Practicing vulnerability can significantly shift how you view yourself and interact with others. It transforms interactions from superficial exchanges to meaningful connections. It changes self-perception from one of isolation and inadequacy to one of authenticity and belonging. By embracing vulnerability, you learn to love yourself and engage more openly and honestly with the world. Cultivating environments and relationships where vulnerability is respected and reciprocated is vital. This openness is not without risk but is also the pathway to more profound love, connection, and authenticity. As you learn to embrace your vulnerabilities, you may find they are not the weaknesses you feared but doorways to a more compassionate and fulfilling life.

Embracing vulnerability is, therefore, not just about sharing and openness; it is an ongoing process of accepting who you are and allowing yourself to grow from experiences that may initially seem daunting. It is about changing the narrative from vulnerability as a weakness to vulnerability as a strength—a core component of loving and understanding yourself deeply. This shift is subtle yet profound, as it touches the essence of how we interact with ourselves and the world around us. It requires courage and persistence but is greatly rewarded with happiness and love.

"I'm still working on self-love. I feel like I just realized in the last six months that I'm the problem. I used to think of myself as this great person with great morals and values, and everyone else was f***ed up. I was the judge and the jury, and I was a runner. So, I'm facing all the things I need to change, and I just stopped drinking. Like, I haven't had a drink in 21 days! So now I'm facing my shadows and hoping to come out on the other side of it with more self-love."

Courtney

Practical Exercise: Share an Untold Story with a Friend

- Reflect on a story you haven't shared with many people. Then, find a trusted friend and tell them that story. Vulnerability is the birthplace of self-love. Tell them about your weaknesses as well as your strengths, ability to overcome struggles and suffering, and courage to keep going!

CHAPTER 3:

Self-Care: Daily Practices for Self-Love

A natural evolution of increasing self-love is initiating self-care practices that deeply nourish and care for yourself. Why wouldn't you give yourself every wonderful thing you need when you love yourself? Imagine greeting each morning not as a series of tasks to be checked off but as a sacred opportunity to set a tone of self-love and care that echoes throughout your day. What does your self-care look like when you love yourself? How do you eat, rest, and nurture yourself with loving relationships and interactions? How do you nurture your body, mind, and spirit? Imagine the kind of self-care that nourishes and cares for you after a hard day. This chapter will explore self-care practices tailored to you.

"I love taking good care of myself."

Morning Rituals for a Self-Loving Start

Creating a morning routine is akin to laying down a garden path of intentions; each step taken on this path reinforces your commitment to nurturing your well-being. The beauty of a morning routine lies in its ability to transform ordinary acts into profound expressions of self-love, turning the simple act of rising from bed into a deliberate practice of self-affirmation. This ritualistic approach to beginning your day helps ground your thoughts and emotions, providing a stable base to navigate the day's complexities with grace and presence.

Consider incorporating practices such as meditation, stretching, or saying positive affirmations in front of a mirror into your morning routine. Meditation, even if practiced for just a few minutes, can significantly decrease stress and increase your overall sense of well-being. Sit quietly and paying attention to your thoughts, breathing, or sensations without judgment, thereby allowing yourself to start your day with a clear and centered mind. Stretching gently awakens your body, enhances physical flexibility, and signals respect for your body's needs. Meanwhile, positive affirmations can fortify your self-esteem and combat negative thinking patterns. Phrases like "I am worthy of good things" or "I receive love effortlessly" can profoundly impact your mindset, rooting your day in self-love.

Successful people across diverse fields support the physical and psychological benefits of a morning routine. Research indicates that consistent morning rituals can enhance mental health, boost productivity, and even contribute to a greater sense of life satisfaction. These routines can lower morning cortisol levels, making stress more manageable and allowing you to approach your day with a calm, focused attitude. Moreover, the predictability of a morning routine can provide comfort, reducing anxiety about the unknown and fortifying you against the day's unpredictability.

In embracing these morning rituals, you do more than start your day; you reaffirm your worth and set a precedent for self-love and care that influences all aspects of your life. Each morning becomes a renewal of your commitment to yourself, a daily declaration of your value and your values. These practices prepare you for the day ahead and a richer, more compassionate life.

"In the morning after I've had my coffee, I do something called HeartMath. I breathe in to the count of five and breathe out to the count of five and focus on feelings of love and appreciation. I usually emanate love and appreciation out to my tiny little chihuahua. She is so easy to love! It makes me feel so regulated and calm when I do that every morning. It's one of the ways I take care of myself."

Catherine

Exercise: Personalization of Your Morning Ritual

- Take a few moments to consider or write down what a morning ritual tailored explicitly to your self-care needs and lifestyle would look like. What makes you feel most at peace and energized in the morning? Do you prefer quiet solitude with coffee, or do you find energy in a brisk morning walk, stretching, and yoga? You may feel most aligned through writing, reading, or activities that stir your soul.

- Once you have identified these activities, consider how they can be realistically integrated into your morning. Block off that time in your calendar or put a reminder on your phone so you don't forget!

Food Preparation and Mindful Eating

In the pursuit of self-care, how we nourish our bodies is just as crucial as how we nourish our minds. Mindful food preparation and eating is a practice that fosters excellent health, but it also promotes a healthier relationship with food and with our bodies. Preparing and consuming meals with intention and attention, focusing entirely on the experience of how we care for ourselves and how we eat, is how we integrate self-care into our daily eating habits. This practice is not just about what we eat but how we eat, encouraging a deep connection to nourishing our bodies and acknowledging the role of food in our well-being.

Preparing food that nourishes your body is a key component of self-care. Not only does your physical health depend on it, but your mental health is dramatically affected by what you put in your body. Eating fast food, processed food, or not eating at regular times creates a state of stress in the body. Loving ourselves with food means thinking in advance about what we should eat, having healthy food in the fridge and pantry, preparing meals regularly that include protein, vegetables, and fruits, as well as including foods that bring us pleasure and joy! Eating good oils, meat, dairy, and organic produce gives us the gift of balanced minds and bodies—what more significant act of self-love could there be? Then, rather than race through eating our food, eating while watching television, or spacing out, we can choose to eat mindfully.

Mindful eating involves several vital steps that create this connection. First, it starts with eating slowly, allowing you to taste and enjoy your food genuinely. Slowing down the pace of your meals can transform eating from a mindless act into a deliberate act of self-care. Each bite becomes an opportunity to connect with the present moment, appreciating the food's flavors, textures, and aromas and the wonderful people who prepared it—including you! This deliberate pacing also aids digestion and can help recognize when you are full, preventing overeating, which often results from rapid, inattentive eating habits to cover up uncomfortable feelings that arise.

Savoring each bite is another cornerstone of mindful eating. It means engaging all your senses to experience your meal fully. Notice the texture of the food, the complexity of flavors, and the aromas that make each dish unique. This practice enhances your enjoyment of the meal and deepens your appreciation for the nourishment it provides. By savoring your food, you affirm the importance of feeding your body with respect and gratitude, reinforcing a positive relationship between eating and your body.

Listening to your body's hunger cues is essential to mindful eating. It involves distinguishing between true hunger and emotional hunger, which prompts eating out of boredom, stress, or other emotional needs. To cultivate this awareness, pause before eating and assess your hunger on a scale from one to ten. This pause helps you recognize whether you are eating out of necessity or habit, guiding you to make choices that are in tune with your body's needs. Sometimes dehydration gives you hunger cues, and your body cries out for water. Ask yourself what your body needs. Is it water, rest, food, or something else?

Linking mindful eating to self-love is intrinsic to the practice. Every choice to eat mindfully affirms your worth and a commitment to your health. It encourages a nurturing approach to food that respects your body's needs and acknowledges its signals. This respectful, attentive approach can significantly combat negative body image, replacing criticism with care. As you practice mindful eating, you learn to treat your body as a cherished vessel deserving of nourishment, respect, and love.

As you continue to explore and integrate mindful eating practices into your life, remember that each meal is an opportunity to reinforce these positive interactions with food and body. Over time, these practices enhance your physical health and deepen your sense of self-love as you learn to nurture your body with attentiveness and respect.

"Eating is one of my self-care rituals. It's how I take time to bring love and pleasure into my life. It lets me know I am lovable and worthy of nurturing and care."

Natasha

Exercise: Practice Mindful Eating

- To integrate mindful eating into your daily routine, practice these two simple exercises that focus on mindfulness during meals.

- **The Gratitude Pause:** Before each meal, pause to express gratitude for the food before you eat it. Consider all the elements and efforts that brought the meal to your table—the ingredients grown by farmers, the transportation that delivered them, the preparation by cooks, or even your efforts in cooking. This pause for gratitude shifts your focus from consuming to appreciating, fostering a more profound respect for your food and its role in your health.

- **The Five Senses Exercise:** Now, take a moment to observe your meal with all five senses. Look at the colors and arrangement of the food on your plate. Touch it to feel the texture. Listen to any sounds it makes, from sizzle to crunch. Smell the aromas, and finally, taste it thoughtfully. This exercise not only enhances the sensory experience of eating but also grounds you in the present moment, making you more aware of the act of eating. Enjoy!

Mindfulness Basics for Daily Self-Love

Mindfulness, in its essence, is the practice of being present and engaged with whatever we are doing now. Non-attachment, a fundamental principle in mindfulness, involves observing your thoughts and feelings without clinging to them or allowing them to dictate your actions. Practicing non-attachment encourages mental and emotional flexibility, helping us respond to life's challenges with greater calm and less distress. Mindfulness is a profound method to cultivate self-love as it teaches us to appreciate our moment-to-moment experiences and not be overwhelmed by what could have been or should be. This acceptance and presence are at the heart of self-love, allowing us to appreciate ourselves as we are.

The role of mindfulness in emotional processing is pivotal. It allows you to observe your emotional reactions without judgment, providing a safe space to fully acknowledge and experience your feelings. This observational stance is essential for the safe and constructive release of emotions. Instead of suppressing or being overwhelmed by feelings, mindfulness gives you the tools to understand and work through them. For instance, if you experience a surge of anger, mindfulness allows you to recognize it, explore its origins, and decide how to respond in a way that aligns with your values and needs rather than reacting impulsively.

The practice of mindfulness can start with something as simple as breathing techniques. One essential yet powerful practice is mindful breathing, where you focus solely on your breath, the inhale and exhale. You can do this anywhere and anytime. Observe each breath without trying to adjust it. Notice where you feel your breath in your body; it could be your nose, throat, chest, or stomach. Feel the sensations of each breath and notice the pause between inhalation and exhalation. This practice can anchor you back to the present moment when you are distracted by negative thoughts or overwhelming feelings.

Another accessible practice is mindful observation. This can be done with any object, although natural objects such as plants or trees are often recommended due to their soothing properties. Select an object within your immediate environment and focus on watching it for a minute or two. Notice its colors, shapes, textures, and any movement it might have. Allow yourself to be consumed by its presence; this can help enhance your attention to detail and reduce stress, fostering a calm and connected state of mind.

Mindfulness not only helps in reducing stress but is also a powerful tool for emotional regulation. By practicing mindfulness, you are training your brain to stay in the present. This helps reduce the kind of rumination that often leads to anxiety and depression. Regular mindfulness practice, even a few minutes a day, has been shown to decrease the activity in our amygdala—the part of our brain responsible for processing stress, fear, and emotional responses. By reducing this activity, mindfulness allows us a greater capacity to manage difficult emotions, thereby fostering a sense of peace and stability.

Body scan meditation is another transformative technique that involves mentally scanning your body for areas of tension and consciously releasing them. This practice encourages you to connect with your physical self in a nurturing way, promoting a mindful awareness of bodily sensations and fostering a gentle acceptance of your body. As you progress through the scan, you are encouraged to release physical tension and any emotional burdens you might be carrying. This process can be incredibly liberating, as it often reveals hidden areas of emotional distress manifesting as physical discomfort, allowing for a release and healing that might not be accessible through more cognitive forms of therapy.

Integrating mindfulness into your daily routine can be done seamlessly. It does not necessarily require dedicated blocks of time, which can be challenging to find on a busy day. Instead, it can be incorporated into activities you already do—for example, practice mindfulness during your daily shower. Notice the feel of the water, the scent of the soap, and the sensation of the towel as you dry off. Stay present with the experience and keep bringing your attention back to the sensations of showering when it starts to wander off. This shift can dramatically enhance your relationship with yourself as you learn to be present with and kind to yourself throughout the day.

Consistency in the practice of these mindfulness techniques cannot be overstated. The more profound benefits of mindfulness, including substantial emotional healing, are most often realized through regular, sustained practice. In this way, mindfulness acts not just as a practice but as a lifestyle, a profound way to cultivate deeper self-love and acceptance. Over time, as these practices become a natural part of your daily life, they not only ease day-to-day stress, but also foster a more profound, compassionate acceptance of yourself and your emotional landscape. As you continue to practice, you might discover that the most significant shifts occur not during meditation but in the moments in between—when you find yourself responding to challenges with unexpected calm, approaching yourself and others with more profound compassion, or simply noticing the beauty in a previously mundane moment. These are the signs of deep emotional healing in action, facilitated by your commitment to mindfulness practices.

"Self-love for me is prioritizing my needs and spiritual growth."

Cinthia

Exercise: Mindfulness Practice

- Select one of the above mindfulness exercises, set a timer, and practice it for five minutes.

- Notice how your body and mind feel at the end of five minutes.

- If you're curious about mindfulness, try a second exercise.

- Consider setting a regular time each day for mindfulness, even if it's just for a few minutes during your morning routine or at night before bed. You can download a mindfulness bell to remind you to practice at your time of choice!

Saying No to Social Media Comparison

In today's digital age, social media platforms have become an integral part of our daily routines. While these platforms offer unprecedented opportunities for connection and engagement, they also present a unique set of psychological challenges, particularly the tendency for social media comparison. Understanding why we compare ourselves to others on these platforms can provide valuable insights into managing these feelings and using social media more healthfully.

Humans are innately social creatures, and our brains are wired to gauge our community standing. Social media amplifies this instinct by providing constant access to snapshots of others' lives, which often appear more glamorous or fulfilled than they actually are. This comparison is skewed further by the highly curated nature of social media, where individuals selectively share highlights of their lives, often adorned with filters and edits that enhance the appeal. This distortion creates an environment where your everyday reality seems dull or inadequate in contrast to the idealized lives you see online, which can perpetuate feelings of envy, inadequacy, and lowered self-esteem.

Developing strategies that help manage how and when you engage with these platforms is crucial to combat the adverse effects of social media comparison. Setting time limits on social media use is a straightforward yet effective way to reduce exposure to potentially harmful content. Many smartphones and digital devices now offer tools that track your usage and allow you to set limits on specific apps, helping you become more conscious of your online time and encouraging healthier habits.

Taking regular digital detoxes can also be beneficial. This involves intentionally setting aside hours, days, or weeks where you log off from social media and digital communications. These breaks can help reset your perspective, reducing the urge to compare and increase appreciation for your life without the constant backdrop of others' curated experiences. During these detox periods, engage in activities you enjoy and provide fulfillment, such as reading, exercising, or spending time in nature. These activities divert your attention from digital distractions and enhance your mood and self-esteem through productive and enjoyable experiences.

It's also essential to cultivate and nurture real-life relationships. While social media can provide a sense of connection, it's often superficial and lacks the depth of face-to-face interactions. Investing time and energy in building strong, supportive relationships in the real world can provide a more substantial and fulfilling sense of community and belonging. Engage regularly with friends and family members through direct interactions, such as having meals together, participating in group activities, or simply talking and catching up in person. These interactions are vital for emotional health and can provide a more accurate reflection of mutual support and genuine connection, free from social media distortions.

By understanding the psychological triggers of social media comparison and implementing strategies to mitigate its effects, you can enjoy the benefits of digital connectivity without falling into the comparison trap. Remember, the key is mindful consumption—being aware of how social media affects your feelings and taking proactive steps to manage your engagement with these platforms. Through mindful practice and active participation in the real world, you can foster a healthier, more balanced approach to social media, enhancing your overall well-being and satisfaction with life.

"I personally just had to get off Instagram and Facebook. It never made me feel good to be on there. I'd just get sucked in and compare myself to other people! That never made me feel very good about myself."

Laura

Exercise: Social Media Purge

- If you currently use social media, take ten minutes and clean up your social media in a way that feels good to you. Maybe you delete some apps or unfollow some "friends" whose posts trigger unpleasant feelings, self-comparison, or jealousy. You can even download apps that limit your time if that's what you prefer.

- Then, reach out to friends to set up some real-life activities like hiking, cooking together, or a day trip somewhere fun!

Creating a Self-Love Playlist for Daily Movement

Music, in its diverse forms, holds the remarkable power to influence our mood and self-perception. It can act as a catalyst for emotional release or a soothing balm for our anxieties, echoing our deepest feelings and amplifying our triumphant moments. The right melody can lift our spirits, and specific lyrics can resonate with our experiences, providing solace and motivation. This emotional impact of music on our psyche is why creating a self-love playlist is a profoundly personal and powerful tool for nurturing a positive relationship with oneself.

Utilizing a playlist to motivate us to move daily is also a great act of self-love and self-care. Physical activity benefits our physical health and is crucial in nurturing our mental and emotional well-being. When we exercise through structured workouts, yoga, dancing, or simply walking, we actively show ourselves care and respect. Movement allows us to connect with our bodies, fostering a more profound awareness and appreciation for what our bodies can achieve. This process of movement and exercise can be a powerful form of self-love, promoting feelings of accomplishment, reducing stress, and boosting our mood by releasing endorphins. Integrating regular physical activity into our lives improves physical fitness and strengthens our self-esteem and self-love.

When selecting songs for your self-love playlist, it's vital to choose music that uplifts and inspires you or resonates with your journey toward self-love. Think about songs that have touched you deeply or make you feel understood or empowered. These could be songs that remind you of a particular achievement or a time when you felt exceptionally joyful. Alternatively, they might be melodies that speak of resilience and overcoming challenges, echoing the struggles and triumphs on the path to self-love. Each song you choose should reflect the feelings and mindsets you wish to cultivate—courage, peace, joy, or self-acceptance.

As you grow and change, so will the music that resonates with you. Make a habit of periodically reviewing and updating your playlist. Add new songs that reflect your current feelings and experiences or remove those that no longer serve your emotional needs. Creating and regularly updating a self-love playlist is a dynamic way to support your emotional well-being and foster a deeper connection with yourself. It allows you to harness the transformative power of music, using it as a tool to cultivate a positive self-image and a loving relationship with yourself. As you curate each song, you are essentially scripting the soundtrack of your life—a soundtrack that empowers, enriches, and uplifts you, accompanying you on your path to self-love.

"Music is one of the ways I calm myself down when I get anxious, especially in the evening. It makes me feel safe. I also have a picture of myself as a baby and each night before I go to bed, I look at that picture and I tell her that she's so beautiful and talented and that I'm so proud of her and I'm always going to protect her. I do that every night before bed."

Lila

Exercise: Music for Self-Love Through Movement

- Create a playlist to support your daily activities and emotional needs.

- Consider listening to your self-love playlist during your morning routine to start your day or play it during your commute to and from work. Workouts are another excellent opportunity to use your playlist, as music can boost your energy levels and enhance your endurance, making your exercise routine more enjoyable and effective.

- When you might be feeling down or struggling with negative thoughts, your self-love playlist can be a handy tool for an emotional boost, helping you realign your worth and strengths.

- Feel like spreading the self-love? Organize a dance party with friends to all your favorite self-love songs. Have everyone contribute three to five of their favorite songs to the party.

Connecting with Nature for Emotional Well-Being

In the fast-paced rhythm of modern life, where concrete replaces greenery and the glow of screens outshines the sunlight, we sometimes forget an essential truth: Humans are intrinsically connected to nature. This connection transcends mere enjoyment of a beautiful landscape and can significantly influence our mental and emotional health. The practice of eco-therapy, which involves engaging with nature to promote well-being, has gained recognition for its profound ability to alleviate stress, enhance mood, and clarify the mind. By integrating eco-therapy into your routine, you nurture your emotional health and reaffirm your bond with the natural world, tapping into a wellspring of tranquility and renewed energy.

The therapeutic benefits of spending time in nature are well-documented. Natural settings have a unique way of engaging our senses, calming the mind, and reducing the physiological symptoms of stress. For instance, studies[5] have shown that walking through a forest can lower blood pressure, decrease levels of the stress hormone cortisol, and improve overall heart health. Furthermore, the serene environment can help clear your mind, improving focus and creativity. Even the simple act of listening to the sounds of a forest or a stream can enhance emotional calm and resilience, providing a much-needed break from the stresses of daily life.

There are numerous ways to connect with nature, regardless of your proximity to wilderness areas. Gardening, for example, is a form of eco-therapy that you can practice in your backyard or urban settings

---

5   Horiuchi M, Endo J, Akatsuka S, Hasegawa T, Yamamoto E, Uno T, Kikuchi S. An effective strategy to reduce blood pressure after forest walking in middle-aged and aged people. J Phys Ther Sci. 2015 Dec;27(12):3711-6. doi: 10.1589/jpts.27.3711. Epub 2015 Dec 28. PMID: 26834337; PMCID: PMC4713776.

via community gardens or window boxes. Tending to plants fosters a connection to the earth and instills a sense of responsibility and accomplishment as you watch your plants grow and thrive. Hiking is another excellent way to engage with nature. It combines physical activity with the sensory pleasure of the natural world, enhancing your physical fitness and emotional well-being. Even something as simple as spending a quiet moment in a park or by a body of water can refresh the mind and spirit.

Our inherent attraction to nature is not just a preference but a fundamental component of our psychological well-being. By fostering this connection through regular interactions with nature, you can enhance your mood, improve mental health, and increase feelings of happiness. Whether watching birds, caring for houseplants, or walking barefoot on grass, small daily interactions with nature can significantly impact your well-being, grounding you in the present moment and reducing feelings of anxiety and depression.

Eco-therapy is not just a practice but a transformative journey that can restore and deepen your connection with the natural world. This bond is essential for personal well-being and the health of our planet. As you step outside and allow nature to envelop you in its tranquility, remember that each breath of fresh air, each step on a forest path, and each moment spent under a canopy of trees is a step toward a more balanced and harmonious life.

"When I go outdoors, I just feel so much love inside of myself. Nature fills me up with so much love. I feel it for everyone and everything, including myself. I can't help but feel good."

Bea

Exercise: Schedule Your Regular Nature Outing

- Think about how you can spend some time each week in nature. Can you sit on your patio and listen to the birds each morning? Start a small container garden that you need to go outdoors to water? Attend an outdoor yoga class in your area or schedule a weekly walk with a friend in the park?

- Put some nature outings in your calendar!

Your Self-Love Language: Self-Care Tailored to You

The concept of the five love languages has transformed numerous relationships, offering insights into how individuals express and prefer to receive love. This framework, developed by Dr. Gary Chapman, identifies five primary ways people show love: words of affirmation, acts of service, receiving gifts, quality time, and physical touch. Interestingly, these languages can also be applied to our relationships with ourselves. Understanding and using your self-love language can significantly enhance how you nurture your emotional needs, leading to a deeper connection with yourself and a stronger foundation of self-love.

To discover your primary self-love language, consider when you feel most cared for or content with yourself. What actions or situations lead to these feelings? For some, taking time to meditate or read a favorite book falls under quality time. For others, it could be preparing a healthy meal, representing acts of service to oneself. Reflect on these experiences and categorize them under the five languages to identify which resonate most strongly with you. This discovery process is about identifying and appreciating the unique ways you feel valued and cared for by yourself!

Once you have identified your primary self-love language, it becomes easier to tailor self-care practices that align with your emotional needs. For those who find that quality time is their self-love language, activities like solo dates, long walks in nature, or quiet mornings spent journaling can be exceptionally fulfilling. If physical touch resonates more, yoga, long baths, self-pleasuring, or self-massage might be more beneficial. Those who respond well to words of affirmation might find it helpful to write affirmations on their mirror or refrigerator or keep a gratitude journal. For acts of service, organizing your living space or scheduling regular health checkups can be acts of self-love. Lastly, if receiving gifts is your self-love language, treating yourself to small gifts like a new book, flowers, or a special meal can be deeply satisfying.

The importance of regularly practicing your self-love language cannot be overstated. Consistency in speaking your self-love language helps reinforce your love for yourself. It acts like watering a plant: Regular care ensures growth and vitality. Moreover, during times of stress or emotional turmoil, leaning into your self-love language can provide comfort and stability, reminding you of your worth and resilience. It is also important to note that while you may have a primary self-love language, incorporating elements from all five can provide a well-rounded approach to self-care, ensuring that your emotional needs are met in various ways.

Incorporating these practices into your life doesn't require grand gestures; instead, small, everyday actions accumulate to foster profound emotional well-being. By understanding and applying your self-love language, you create a personalized blueprint for nurturing yourself that respects and reflects your unique needs and preferences. This approach empowers you to take control of your emotional health and cultivate a loving and compassionate relationship with yourself, which is the essence of self-love. As you continue to explore and integrate these practices into your life, you may find that they enhance your relationship with yourself and others as you become more attuned to the languages of love in all forms.

"My first love language is acts of service—even small ones. I told my husband on our first date that I had just bought my car and was looking for a new mechanic. He didn't say much at the time but on our next date, he brought me the business card for his favorite mechanic. It made me feel so heard. It helped reveal his character to me —one that takes interest in helping others. My self-love language is nature hiking, I suppose—to be out on a long walk where I'm able to unplug from all the obligations and the buzz of technology."

Audrey

Exercise: Find Your Love Language

- Reflect on the five love languages and what actions make you feel the most cared for.

- Get your journal or some paper and write out the five love languages: words of affirmation, acts of service, receiving gifts, quality time, and physical touch. Then, for each language, list two or three examples of loving yourself in that way.

- Post this somewhere you can revisit regularly to remind yourself of the special ways you like to be shown love.

Make a Difference with Your Review

"Be the love you never received."
Rune Lazuli

People who give without expecting anything in return live happier lives. So, let's make a difference together!

Would you help a woman just like you—curious about self-love but unsure where to start?

My mission is to make self-love available for all women!

But to reach more people, I need your help.

Most people choose books based on reviews. So, I'm asking you to help a fellow female reader by leaving a review.

It costs nothing and takes less than a minute but could change someone's self-love journey. Your review could help...

...one more young woman step into loving herself.
...one more mother learn compassionate communication with her children.
...one more grown woman learn to love her body and practice self-care.
...one more woman just like you to love her relationships and her life!

To make a difference, simply scan the QR code and leave a review:
https://www.amazon.com/review/review-your-purchases/?asin=B0DDJPM74L

Thank you!
Lauren Brim, Ph.D.

CHAPTER 4:

Healthy Boundaries and Relationships

We all want to experience healthy relationships, but often, the unhealthy dynamics from childhood will feel familiar, so we'll unconsciously seek them out in our adult relationships. At some level, those familiar relationships feel like love. On our journey of self-love, there comes a moment when our self-worth has increased so much that we start drawing in a different caliber of people who reflect the inner self-worth and state of peace we've worked to cultivate. How we value and treat ourselves sets the tone for how we interact with others, influencing the quality and health of our relationships.

However, on our self-love journey, toxic or abusive relationships can emerge—subtle or overt dynamics that undermine our well-being rather than uplift it. Recognizing and addressing these harmful patterns is essential for our emotional and physical health and fostering relationships that genuinely reflect our worth. Learning to have healthy boundaries is a large part of having healthy relationships, and healthy people will respect those boundaries. This chapter explores how to cultivate healthy relationships with our children, friends, lovers, and birth family are explored in this chapter. Self-love sets the standard for how we let others treat us.

> **"My love for myself is reflected in my relationships. I have healthy boundaries with others."**

Identifying Toxic and Abusive Relationships

The phrase "toxic relationship" has increased in popularity over recent years. A toxic relationship is characterized by behaviors that consistently undermine one's well-being. These relationships can be with a romantic partner, family member, friend, or colleague and typically involve patterns of criticism, manipulation, lack of support, and gaslighting. The roots of why toxic people do this to others are often complex, intertwined with issues of power, insecurity, and deep-seated behavioral patterns. Some also call them abusive relationships, although toxic relationships and abusive relationships are related but not the same.

Toxic Relationship: A toxic relationship generally refers to a relationship that is emotionally damaging or draining for one or both partners. It may involve constant criticism, manipulation, lack of respect for boundaries, and negativity. Toxic relationships can impact one's self-esteem, mental health, and overall well-being; however, they may not always involve clear-cut abuse (physical, sexual, financial, or severe emotional abuse).

Abusive Relationship: An abusive relationship involves behaviors that are intentionally harmful or coercive toward one partner by the other. Abuse can manifest in various forms: physical (hitting, pushing), sexual (coercion, assault), emotional (gaslighting, manipulation), or verbal (name-calling, threats). Abuse is about exerting power and control over the other person, often resulting in fear, harm, and a sense of helplessness for the victim.

All abusive relationships can be considered toxic due to their damaging effects, but not all toxic relationships are necessarily abusive. Both types of relationships are harmful and should be addressed with appropriate support and intervention to protect the well-being of those involved. While abusive behavior is often easier to spot, some examples of toxic behavior include:

1. **Guilt-tripping:** A person might use statements like, "If you really cared about me, you would do this for me," to manipulate someone into doing something they don't want to do, like have sex with them, avoid their responsibilities or give them money.

2. **Gaslighting:** This involves manipulating someone into doubting their perception, memory, or sanity. For example, someone might say, "You're overreacting; that never happened," when the other person recalls an event differently, laugh at their recollection, or call them crazy.

3. **Emotional blackmail:** This occurs when someone threatens to withhold love, approval, or support unless the other person complies with their demands. For instance, "If you leave me, I'll never forgive you," or "If you don't do X, I'll tell everyone you did Y," or "If you loved me, you'd do what I'm telling you to do."

4. **Playing the victim:** Some people constantly portray themselves as victims in situations, attempting to elicit sympathy and support while deflecting responsibility for their actions. These people are usually litigious (so watch out!) and will accuse you of everything they do.

5. **Manipulative praise or criticism:** This involves using compliments or criticisms strategically to control someone's

behavior or emotions. For example, they may praise excessively when they want something or criticize to make someone feel inadequate or insecure. This is often seen early in relationships where the toxic person will overwhelm someone with compliments, known as love-bombing, only to either leave once they've gotten what they wanted, such as sex, or criticize and abuse them in other ways once they've gotten married or had a child together.

6. **Exploiting empathy:** Exploiting someone's empathy involves manipulating their compassion or care for others to get what they want. For instance, they may use a sad story or play on someone's sympathy to gain favors or forgiveness. This often happens when someone wants money from someone or something for free, and they will tell them stories that exploit their empathy to get what they want, like, "My family has nothing to eat," when they are spending all their money on drugs instead of food.

Recognizing these toxic and abusive behaviors is crucial to protecting ourselves and making sure we're in healthy relationships with healthy boundaries. Establishing clear boundaries and communicating with assertiveness is essential in protecting oneself from emotional manipulation. Addressing or exiting toxic relationships necessitates courage, a clear strategy, and sometimes seeking help. Begin by acknowledging the reality of the situation and permitting yourself to seek a healthier environment. This might involve setting boundaries to limit your exposure to toxic behaviors or, in more severe cases, completely severing ties with the individual. Communication is vital in these scenarios—expressing your feelings and experiences can sometimes help the other person recognize the need for change.

However, it's important to approach such conversations cautiously, especially if the relationship has been deeply manipulative. Some people won't change, and it's best you cut ties.

Addressing Toxic Dynamics

For those navigating the complex process of distancing themselves from toxic or abusive relationships, consider these steps:

1. **Document interactions:** Keeping a record can help you see patterns and provide a basis for your feelings and decisions.

2. **Seek support:** Talk to friends, family, or professionals who can offer emotional support and objective advice.

3. **Establish boundaries:** Clearly define what is unacceptable and communicate these boundaries assertively.

4. **Plan for pushback:** Often, individuals in toxic or abusive relationships will resist change. Plan how to handle potential confrontations calmly and safely.

5. **Prioritize self-care:** Reinforce your self-worth through positive affirmations, engaging in activities you love, and reaffirming your strengths and values.

Identifying signs of toxic relationships or emotional abuse is crucial, as many may normalize or dismiss these behaviors, especially if they have been enduring them for an extended period. Common signs that you're in an abusive dynamic include feeling unworthy or inadequate due to constant belittlement, experiencing anxiety or depression that seems connected to a relationship, and feeling like you are walking on eggshells, afraid of triggering a negative reaction. Emotional abuse might also manifest as isolation from friends and family, as abusers often attempt to control and limit victims' interactions with others. Recognizing these signs can be painful but is essential for beginning the healing process.

Therapeutic approaches offer effective means of healing from toxic or abusive relationships. Cognitive behavioral therapy (CBT) is particularly beneficial, as it involves identifying and challenging the distorted thinking patterns that can develop in victims of emotional abuse. CBT helps you recognize and refute the untruths instilled by abusers—such as worthlessness or powerlessness—and replace them with more accurate and empowering beliefs. Trauma-focused therapy, another valuable approach, addresses the specific emotional and psychological trauma resulting from abuse. This type of therapy often involves techniques where you confront and gradually learn to cope with feelings and memories associated with the abuse under the guidance of a trained therapist.

Incorporating self-compassion into your recovery can significantly affect your healing process. Self-compassion involves treating yourself with the same kindness, concern, and support you would offer a good friend. For survivors of emotional abuse, this practice, while not always easy at first, can be transformative. Self-compassion allows you to acknowledge your suffering without judgment and understand that your experiences do not define your worth. Therapy and self-compassion practices provide not only pathways out of the shadow of emotional abuse but also the means to rediscover and reaffirm your sense of self. They equip you with tools to rebuild your self-esteem and engage in relationships with renewed confidence and trust.

Navigating away from toxic or abusive relationships is a significant step toward embracing a life where self-love and respect dictate your interactions. As you move forward, remember that the relationships you nurture should echo the love and respect you cultivate within yourself. This alignment enhances your well-being and attracts and sustains healthier, more fulfilling relationships.

"I experienced more self-love after my breakup with my husband. Suddenly, being single and in charge made me become the untainted version of myself. When I was living with someone else, I didn't think I could live alone; I would receive unsolicited comments about my personality, lack of energy, or beliefs, I would ask others their opinion before making decisions, and I wouldn't take the time to develop new skills. I would rely more on others to do what I couldn't do. Leaving that relationship changed my whole life."

Kendall

Exercise: Evaluating Your Relationships

- Think about the relationships in your life while you review the characteristics of toxic or abusive dynamics. Do you spot any of these dynamics in your relationships?

- Write down the toxic behaviors on the left and to the right, journal about the strategy you feel would be appropriate to distance yourself from those behaviors.

- Prioritize your well-being and happiness and choose to surround yourself with healthy, loving dynamics as much as possible.

Healing from Negativity in Family Dynamics

Family dynamics play a crucial role in shaping who we are, influencing how we view ourselves and our emotional well-being from a young age. The family unit, often our first social group, teaches us how to relate to ourselves and others. Unfortunately, not all these lessons are positive. Negative family dynamics, such as persistent criticism, lack of emotional support, or controlling behaviors, can profoundly affect our self-esteem and emotional health. These dynamics can leave us feeling inadequate, overly self-critical, or fearful of expressing our true selves. Understanding how these familial interactions have shaped our perception of ourselves is pivotal in initiating the healing process.

One effective way to mitigate the impact of negative family dynamics is through emotional separation. This involves creating psychological boundaries between yourself and family members who perpetuate negativity. Emotional separation allows you to interact with these family members without letting their words or actions dictate your feelings about yourself. It involves recognizing that their behavior reflects their struggles and insecurities, not your worth or capabilities. Techniques such as visualization can aid in this process. For instance, imagine a shield around you during interactions, protecting you from negative emotions and preserving your inner peace. This mental image can help reinforce your boundaries, making it easier to maintain your emotional equilibrium in challenging family situations.

Additionally, assertive communication is vital in establishing and maintaining these boundaries. It involves stating your needs and feelings without aggression or passivity. For example, suppose a family member constantly criticizes your career choices. In that case, you might assertively respond, "I understand your concern, but I am happy with my decisions and would appreciate your support or understanding." This kind of communication sets clear boundaries and fosters respect and understanding within the family.

Another transformative approach is redefining your role within your family. Many of us unconsciously take on roles that our families assign us—the peacemaker, the caretaker, the black sheep—and these roles can limit our growth and self-expression. You can redefine yourself outside those preconceived boundaries by consciously choosing which roles to accept and which to let go. Identify your roles and ask yourself how they have impacted your self-esteem and relationships. Decide which aspects of these roles you want to change or release and envision yourself stepping into a new role that is more aligned with who you want to be. This might mean setting new expectations with your family about what you will and won't do, or it could involve changing the way you interact with family members to reflect your true self more authentically.

For those who continue to face negativity from family dynamics, building a chosen family can provide the emotional security and affirmation that biological relatives may not offer. A chosen family is made up of individuals who deliberately choose to play significant roles in each other's lives, and these relationships are based on mutual respect, love, and support. Cultivating a chosen family involves building relationships with friends, mentors, or community members who align with your values and offer the emotional connection and encouragement you deserve. Look for people who nurture your strengths, respect your boundaries, and encourage personal growth. As you build these relationships, invest time and energy in them, just as you would with biological family members, to create solid and enduring bonds.

By understanding the impact of family dynamics, employing strategies for emotional separation, redefining familial roles, and building a supportive chosen family, you empower yourself to overcome the negativity that may have shadowed your family interactions. Creating and maintaining a chosen family enriches your social and emotional life and reinforces your sense of self-worth and belonging. This network of intentional relationships can provide a solid foundation of support, particularly when navigating difficulties with biological family members. It serves as a reminder that family is not solely defined by blood but by the bonds you choose to cultivate and maintain.

"I think I really struggled with self-love because I never felt like my dad loved me. As an adult, he never visited me, which hurt a lot. I also felt like he would turn against me suddenly, even though I felt like I was being the perfect daughter. I didn't remember him spending much time with me as a child or making me feel very important. So yeah, that was hard, and I think a big reason I was with men who didn't appreciate me for two decades. I was loved, but no one really appreciated or committed to me. I think cherished is a good word. I didn't ever feel cherished. I cried a lot of tears over that. But I think there was a change around the time when I was spending time with a much older man whom I had dated several years before. We were just friends then, and he would share a lot about his relationship with his daughter, who was around 23 at the time. God, did he cherish her! He adored her. He would do anything for her. Drive two hours to move her car for her. He would take her on father-daughter trips. I was like, wow, can men really love their daughters like that? I knew I wanted that love. And I think something changed inside of me. I think the bar got raised. Because that's just what I expected from men in the future, and now I'm with a man like that. I knew the little girl in me deserved to be loved like that, too."

Amanda

Exercise: Energetically Building a Nourishing Family Tree

- Grab a piece of paper and draw out your family tree as far back as you can go.

- Now, close your eyes and take some time to imagine life force flowing down to you from your ancestors. Imagine all their love and wisdom pouring into you.

- Then, look at your immediate family relationships in your mind's eye and see if they are a source of support or if they feel weighed down by negativity. If a relationship feels heavy or negative, imagine that person slowly moving away from you just enough so that it feels lighter. You are not necessarily eliminating them from your life, but shifting them to the left or right so someone else can move closer. You can also envision turning them away from you, your children, or your spouse.

- Lastly, envision chosen family members moving closer to you that make you feel supported and loved.

Setting Boundaries: A Step-by-Step Guide

In the intricate landscape of personal relationships and daily interactions, setting boundaries is akin to drawing a map of your emotional needs and limits. Boundaries are essential for maintaining self-respect and protecting your emotional well-being. They act as guidelines or rules that you establish to let people know how they can treat you—what is acceptable and what is not. This clarity is crucial in personal interactions and professional environments, helping to prevent burnout and reduce stress. Boundaries affirm your right to emotional space and are a testament to your self-value.

The first step in effective boundary-setting is identifying where and when you need them. This often involves introspection and reflection on past situations that made you uncomfortable, disrespected, or overwhelmed. For example, if you find yourself routinely staying late at work at the expense of your time, you need a boundary around your work hours. Similarly, if specific conversations with a friend leave you feeling drained or upset, it might be time to set boundaries around the topics you are willing to discuss. The key here is to listen to your feelings and recognize situations where your limits are tested.

Once you've identified these areas, the next step is to communicate your boundaries. This can be challenging, especially if you fear the other person's reaction. However, clear communication is vital for setting boundaries that are respected. Use "I" statements to express your needs and feelings without sounding accusatory, which can help keep the conversation nonconfrontational. For example, instead of saying, "You're always dumping your problems on me," try, "I feel overwhelmed when we discuss stressful topics. I need to focus on positive things right now." This approach doesn't blame the other person but instead focuses on your needs and feelings.

Handling pushback is another critical aspect of setting boundaries. When you first set boundaries, it is common for others to test or push against them, mainly if they are used to the old dynamics of your relationship. They might feel hurt or rejected and express anger or disappointment. Staying firm in such situations and reaffirming your boundaries with calm and consistent responses is essential. Remember, setting boundaries is not about controlling others but about managing your emotional health. If someone continually disrespects your boundaries, reevaluating the relationship and considering more significant changes, such as limiting contact, may be necessary.

Consistency is the glue that holds boundaries in place. Maintaining boundaries can be just as challenging as setting them, especially under pressure when it might seem easier to give in. However, whenever you uphold a boundary, you reinforce your self-respect and ensure your emotional needs are met. To stay consistent, remind yourself of the reasons you set these boundaries in the first place. It can also be helpful to have a support system—friends or family members who understand and support your boundaries, offering encouragement when it becomes challenging to maintain them.

In cultivating a life where your boundaries are recognized and respected, you empower yourself to interact with the world in a healthier and more balanced way. This empowerment allows you to engage in relationships and activities that align with your values and needs, enhancing your quality of life and relationships. As you continue to navigate the complexities of interactions and relationships, remember that setting and maintaining boundaries is a dynamic process that requires flexibility and adaptation as your needs and circumstances evolve. Each step in this process is a step toward a more empowered and fulfilling life where your needs are acknowledged, and your emotional well-being is protected.

"Self-love is always a tough one. I am forever learning to understand who I am, what my needs are, and my values and principles. You have to know yourself before you can love yourself, right? I've had different experiences throughout my life that have helped me grow to love myself. It's not a one-time-experience deal. In my younger years, I was a people pleaser at work and with friends. I finally had enough confidence to ask for what I was worth at work, which was a form of self-love. It's been the same with friends along the way, always wanting to do what's best for them, listening to them for hours and never thinking about myself. This always led to illness and limitations in my life. When I learned to stop being a sounding board for them (thinking I was a loving person) and speak up that it's not beneficial for me to always take on their drama when there was no exchange or balance in the relationship, I gained more energy and integrity. This is an example of self-love. I acknowledged myself, my wants and needs. Every lesson I've had of learning boundaries in self-love for me in the past helps me spot sooner when I am falling into the trap of needing another's love to fill up love for myself. I stand up for myself more quickly because I have learned to honor and respect and love myself more."

Candace

Exercise: Practice Boundaries

- Find a safe person and ask if you can practice communicating boundaries with them.

- Think about a boundary with someone you failed to communicate because it made you uncomfortable.

- Ask your safe person to agree to your boundary when you speak so you can rewire your mind to believe communicating boundaries is safe. Extra credit if they can respond with something validating such as "That totally makes sense."

- Now communicate your boundary to your safe person.

- Notice how your body feels when your boundaries are respected and heard.

- Now practice saying it a few more times, or practice communicating some other boundaries to your safe person.

- Now switch and practice being the one that receives someone's boundaries. If this brings up uncomfortable feelings, just breathe, and keep going. You must get good at creating and respecting boundaries to have healthy relationships.

Communication Skills for Self-Respect and Love

Effective communication is the bedrock upon which strong relationships are built, and it is equally crucial in nurturing self-respect and self-love. Essential communication skills such as active listening, assertiveness, and the correct use of non-verbal cues not only enhance your interactions with others but also reinforce your self-worth by ensuring your voice is heard and your boundaries respected. Active listening involves fully concentrating on what is being said rather than passively hearing the message of the speaker. This skill requires you to listen with all senses and to provide feedback that you comprehend the message accurately. The practice of active listening demonstrates respect for the speaker and can help in building trust in any relationship, fostering a deeper connection and understanding.

Assertiveness is another critical communication skill, particularly when it comes to advocating for your own needs and desires. Being assertive means expressing your thoughts, feelings, and needs openly, honestly, and respectfully. It allows you to communicate without resorting to passive or aggressive behaviors, which can undermine your self-esteem and the health of your relationships. For instance, if a colleague continuously imposes on your time, an assertive response could be, "I understand you need support on this project, but I need to focus on my tasks this afternoon. Can we find another time to discuss this?" This kind of communication respects your boundaries and the other person's needs.

Non-verbal cues, such as eye contact, body posture, and facial expressions, also play a significant role in communication. These cues can often convey more than words and are essential in expressing empathy and understanding. For example, nodding your head while someone is speaking can signal that you are engaged and empathetic, reinforcing a supportive communication environment.

Empathy is a powerful tool in effective communication. It involves understanding and sharing the feelings of another person. Empathy can profoundly impact the depth of your relationships, but before one can experience empathy for another, they must first be able to identify and acknowledge their own painful feelings. How can you relate to another's sadness, anger, or disappointment if you can't identify and feel empathy for your own emotional experiences? Self-empathy is the foundation of empathy for others and involves treating yourself with the same kindness and understanding you desire from others. When you learn to give this to yourself, practice giving it to others in difficult moments through empathetic communication, where you communicate understanding of what they're going through.

Empathetic communication allows you to connect with others deeply, facilitating a shared understanding that can defuse conflicts and build stronger bonds. For example, if a friend is going through a tough time, expressing empathy might sound like, "I see how you're really overwhelmed with this situation. I'm here for you if you need to talk." Or "I see how much you're grieving, and I'm so sorry. This is such a big loss." This empathetic response validates their feelings and shows that you care, strengthening the relationship.

Sometimes, it may not be easy to feel empathy for what someone's going through or to be able to extend this understanding to ourselves. In such a moment, the best we can do is offer validation. Validation is recognition or affirmation that a person or their feelings or opinions are valid or worthwhile. It's a communication skill that helps both parties feel heard and understood. When extending validation to ourselves, this may look like pausing and acknowledging what we are feeling as real. "I feel terrified right now." Or "I am experiencing a lot of overwhelm right now, and it doesn't feel like I should go out tonight." Validating what we're feeling acknowledges that it's real, helps us feel seen, and ultimately helps us move beyond the emotion and take the action we need to take.

Extending validation to those we're in relationship with is a powerful tool to help with a wide range of communications, such as de-escalating high emotions or moving an ordinary everyday conversation along. "You're excited to pick up Danielle at ballet tonight—that's great!" or "I see you're frustrated, babe, and you have every right to feel that way. Your boss is being a jerk."

These may sound simple and redundant, but validating or repeating what someone is experiencing will make them feel connected to you and strengthen the relationship. Sometimes, though, when it's hard to have empathy because a situation or someone's emotion triggers us, all we can do is validate in the most neutral way possible or find one tiny thing in what they're saying that we can validate before moving forward with what we want to say. This may sound like, "I hear that you felt criticized when I said that," or "I see that you're really angry right now." Validation is essential in all relationships, including how we relate to ourselves.

Handling difficult conversations with dignity and respect is essential in maintaining self-respect and strong relationships. Here are specific phrases and techniques that can help you navigate these situations:

1. **When disagreeing with someone's opinion:** "I see your point, but I have a different perspective. May I share my

thoughts?" This approach respects the other person's viewpoint while clearly stating your disagreement.

2. **When needing to set a boundary:** "I value our time together, but I need to make sure I have enough time for other commitments. Let's plan our meetings more efficiently." This script helps you set boundaries respectfully, emphasizing the value of the relationship while asserting your needs.

3. **When giving feedback on sensitive issues:** "I appreciate your efforts on this project. I think we could improve even further by considering some changes. Can we discuss this a bit more?" By starting with appreciation, the feedback is framed positively, making the recipient more receptive to discussion.

4. **When you need to decline a request:** "Thank you for thinking of me for this opportunity, but I cannot commit to this at the moment due to other priorities." This response allows you to decline respectfully, acknowledging the request positively while being clear about your limitations.

By integrating these communication techniques into your daily interactions, you ensure that your conversations reflect and enhance your self-love and respect. This improves your relationships with others and deepens your relationship with yourself as you consistently affirm your worth and ensure your voice is heard. Through clear, assertive, and empathetic communication, you create a life where your needs are respected, your emotions are validated, and your relationships are fulfilling and supportive.

"I think, sometimes, loving yourself is just saying 'No.' No to the things you don't want to do. No to what you usually do to make other people happy. No, thank you. Those are powerful words. I don't think I was taught those words growing up. But you have to be able to say no to take care of yourself. I'm definitely teaching my daughter how to say no. And my son, too!"

Gina

Exercise: Upgrade Your Communication Skills

- Find a friend with whom to practice your communication skills, specifically empathy and validation.

- Sit across from one another or give each other your full attention over the phone. Have one person tell the other something emotionally charged that's happening in their life right now.

- When they are finished, the other person will 1) find something to validate about what they are hearing and 2) find something around which they can express empathy around.

- Now switch roles.

- Notice the feelings that come up and keep practicing until you feel confident in your new skills.

- Note: Resist the urge to offer a solution to their problem. Just validate and empathize!

  Examples of a validating or empathic response:
  Person A: "I'm very stressed that my husband isn't making enough money this summer."
  Person B: "I hear that your husband isn't making enough money, and it's stressing you out. I'm so sorry to hear that. That must be so scary and overwhelming!"

The Role of Self-Love in Romantic Relationships

Most of us experience some of our most significant challenges in romantic relationships. Our partner acts as a mirror for our emotional wounds and some of our best qualities. The presence of self-love in a romantic relationship enhances our well-being and fortifies the bonds shared with a partner. Our partner can reflect the love we've cultivated with ourselves. Growing a deep, abiding love for ourselves is a wellspring of confidence and contentment from which we can more freely give and receive affection. Without this foundation of self-love and self-respect, relationships can often devolve into a minefield of insecurity, dependency, and jealousy, each stemming from an inner void one hopes to fill with external validation.

A robust sense of self-love not only positively impacts romantic partnerships, but also plays a crucial role in fostering a climate of mutual respect and admiration. It encourages partners to see each other as complete individuals on their paths rather than mere extensions of themselves or as means to fulfill personal deficiencies. This perspective deepens intimacy and buffers the relationship against everyday conflicts and misunderstandings. When you appreciate your worth, you are less likely to tolerate or perpetuate demeaning behaviors. This self-respect sets a standard for how you expect to be treated, making you feel more valued and appreciated. Naturally, it elevates how you treat your partner, fostering a cycle of positive regard and behavior.

However, relationships without this bedrock of self-love can often succumb to pitfalls such as dependency, where one partner leans too heavily on the other for their emotional well-being, or jealousy, which can stem from insecurities about one's value and the fear of being replaced or abandoned. Insecurity, a close cousin to jealousy, can lead to possessiveness, a need for constant reassurance, and difficulty trusting one's partner, all of which can undermine the relationship's stability and the individual's psychological health. A lack of self-love can also show up as shame around one's sexuality. Shame can lead to the sexual shutdown of one partner and a lack of necessary intimacy in a romantic relationship.

Engaging in practices that cultivate self-love within the relationship is essential to counteract these challenges. Activities such as joint meditation or couple's therapy can be instrumental. These shared experiences foster self-love and enhance mutual understanding and empathy, strengthening the relationship's foundation. Setting aside time for personal reflection or individual therapy can also be beneficial. Through activities like journaling or working with a therapist or healer, individuals can explore their feelings and thoughts independently, which helps maintain a healthy perspective on the relationship and personal identity. Emotions like shame, fear, and anger need to be examined and released in the individual in order to show up for a healthy, balanced, and passionate romantic relationship.

An equally crucial aspect of nurturing romantic relationships through self-love is encouraging individual growth. Partners need to support each other's personal interests and goals, as this promotes a dynamic and stimulating relationship and reduces the likelihood of resentment or stagnation. By championing each other's pursuits, whether professional aspirations, hobbies, or personal wellness goals, partners can maintain an atmosphere of encouragement and admiration. This support for individual growth demonstrates a love that values the partner's happiness and fulfillment as much as one's own. This approach solidifies the relationship and builds lasting respect and admiration between partners. As you and your partner continue to foster this culture of mutual respect, affection, and encouragement, you'll find that your relationship becomes a robust, supportive framework capable of withstanding the vicissitudes of life while providing a source of joy and fulfillment.

"I was looking for a partner for the longest time. I finally started to try for a baby on my own since it seemed like it wasn't in the cards for me to have a partner. I at least wanted a baby! And I was successful in my career, so I had the money to do it alone. So, I began the insemination process. And when I went in for the insemination, they accidentally injected me with formaldehyde, and I almost died on the table! So that dream ended, and I just went back to living my life and working on the relationship with myself. Then one weekend, I was out of town, and I met this incredibly sexy man, and we had sex all weekend, and I thought, "Well, that was fun. And that's probably all it will be." But he never stopped calling me! It's been five years, and we're married now, and we have a wonderful relationship. We're both too old to have kids, but I have the most incredible husband, and all the work I did on myself before meeting him, I believe, was why I was ready to receive that relationship when I did."

Cindy

Exercise: Improving Your Romantic Relationship

- Take some time to reflect on what practical steps you can take to enhance your relationship with yourself to improve your romantic relationship. Go for more walks in nature? Schedule time with friends? Start working out more regularly? Prepare healthier meals at the start of the week? What would fill up your self-love cup to help you be a better partner?

- Reflect on what you and your partner can do together to improve the health of the relationship? Setting aside more time to talk and connect? Scheduling time for touch and intimacy? Meditating together or attending a workshop as a couple? What would help you both grow in the relationship together?

- Reflect on what you can do to support your partner's individual growth. Do they need more encouragement? Maybe you offer to take the kids out of the house once a week so they can have some alone time in the home? If you can't think of anything, ask them what they need. You might be surprised.

Cultivating a Supportive Friend Network

Friendships enrich our lives, providing joy, companionship, and support. They are the pillars upon which we lean during turbulent times and the cheerleaders who celebrate our victories, big and small. Understanding the qualities that make a friendship truly supportive can significantly enhance your ability to cultivate enduring relationships and actively contribute to your self-love and emotional well-being.

A mutual exchange of affection, respect, and encouragement characterizes a supportive friendship. These relationships are built on trust and emotional safety, where one can share vulnerably without fear of judgment. In a genuinely supportive friendship, there is an intrinsic understanding that the well-being of both parties is essential, and efforts are made to ensure that each person feels valued and heard. Such friendships enrich our lives, providing companionship and a mirror with which we can see the best versions of ourselves reflected.

To cultivate such enriching relationships, it is crucial to assess your current friendships. Reflect on which interactions uplift you and which seem to drain your energy. Consider the balance of give and take in your relationships; supportive friendships typically involve a relatively equal exchange of emotional support. If you find that a friend consistently relies on you without reciprocating or that interactions often leave you feeling worse rather than better, these may be signs that the friendship is not as supportive as it could be. On the other hand, friends who encourage your growth, respect your boundaries, and are present through life's ups and downs are worth keeping.

Finding new friends who elevate and support you can also enhance your network. Engage in activities that align with your interests and values, as these settings can be fertile ground for meeting like-minded individuals. Whether it's a book club, a fitness class, or a volunteer organization, these environments allow you to connect with others who share your passions and outlook on life. When meeting potential friends, be open about your interests and values from the outset. This transparency will help attract people who resonate with your authentic self.

Nurturing these friendships requires regular effort and communication. Like any meaningful relationship, friendships thrive on attention and care. Make time to connect through regular outings, phone calls, or messages. Sharing experiences, from everyday occurrences to significant life events, keeps the bond and mutual support alive. Celebrating each other's successes and being present during challenges is also essential. Showing up for your friends in a way that honors their needs and your own is a cornerstone of supportive friendships.

However, as life evolves, so do our relationships. You might find that certain friendships no longer align with your journey. Perhaps you've grown in different directions, or the relationship dynamics have changed. Recognizing when a friendship no longer serves your well-being is as crucial as nurturing one that does. In this situation, approach the transition with honesty and compassion. Communicate your feelings openly, express gratitude for the friendship, and explain your need to step back. This conversation, while challenging, is often necessary to honor the path of growth and change you are navigating.

A network of supportive friends acts as a source of joy and comfort, and a reflective surface that helps us see and appreciate our best selves. By intentionally choosing and nurturing these relationships, you ensure that your social circle mirrors the love, respect, and kindness you are committed to providing yourself.

"I had a friend in my mid-twenties who I thought really loved me. We did everything together and traveled twice out of the country on amazing trips. But in the end, she left without any warning and never spoke to me again. I grieved that lost friendship for such a long time, but when I look back now, my friendships, just like romantic relationships, were reflecting my relationship with myself. I would abandon myself back then just as easily as she abandoned me. But I've grown and changed a lot since then, and my friendships are really solid now. Even if we don't see each other often, we are there for each other no matter what!"

Audrey

Exercise: Evaluating Your Friendships

- Take a few moments to reflect or journal on your friendships. What are your friendships reflecting about your own self-love? How could you be a better friend? Are there any friendships you'd like to cut out of your life? Or friendships you'd like to invest more in? What does a loving friendship look like?

Parenting with Self-Love and Compassion

Parenting is an intricate dance of guidance, support, boundaries, and, most importantly, love. Self-love, a core component of your emotional and mental well-being, plays a pivotal role in how you parent, which informs the emotional development of your children. When you approach parenting with self-love, you naturally foster a nurturing environment that supports healthy, confident, and emotionally savvy children. Understanding and practicing self-love enhances your parenting skills and teaches your children the importance of loving and respecting themselves.

The influence of self-love on parenting extends to everyday interactions and decisions. When you value yourself, you are more likely to engage in parenting practices that are respectful and understanding rather than reactive or punitive. This approach fosters a household atmosphere where children feel valued and understood, mirroring the respect and love they observe in their parents. Furthermore, when parents handle their emotions compassionately, they set a powerful example for their children, who learn to treat themselves and others with kindness.

Maintaining your emotional well-being while managing your responsibilities and the chaos of parenting can be complex. Self-care is often one of the first things to be neglected by busy parents, but its importance cannot be overstated! Prioritizing self-care can significantly impact your ability to stay balanced and responsive and parent from a place of self-love. First, you must regularly set aside time for activities that replenish your energy and bring you joy, whether it's pursuing a hobby, exercising, calling a friend, or finding quiet time to read or meditate. Establishing a daily or weekly routine that includes these activities can help ensure they don't get pushed out of your schedule by the demands of your children, household, or job. Second, you must have good boundaries and ask for what you need, whether that is asking more from your partner, hiring help, or requiring your children do their part in the household. It takes a village! Lastly, utilizing mindfulness practices or meditation, yoga, or talking with a therapist can enhance your emotional resilience and provide you with tools to manage what is sometimes the overwhelming stress of parenting and show up as a more loving version of yourself.

How we communicate with our children also says much about our relationship with ourselves. Communication is a cornerstone of effective parenting and is deeply enhanced by the practice of compassion. Communicating with your children in ways that foster respect, understanding, and mutual love is essential for their emotional development. This involves actively listening to your children, validating their feelings, and engaging in dialogues that help them articulate their thoughts and emotions. For example, if a child is upset, acknowledge their distress instead of dismissing their feelings as trivial; ask them to describe their feelings and why they feel that way. Then, reflect that back to them. "I hear you're angry that your brother touched your toys." This practice helps children feel heard and valued and teaches them how to express their emotions constructively.

Techniques for Compassionate Communication

1. **Active Listening:** Give your full attention when your child speaks without planning what to say next. Reflect on what you hear to ensure understanding and reinforce that their thoughts are important. Get down on the floor at their level and look them in the eyes.

2. **Empathetic Responses**: Respond to your child's emotions with empathy, understanding, and validation. If they are sad, you might mirror their sadness in your face and tone and say, "It sounds like you're upset about this. It's okay to feel sad. Let's talk about it." Meeting them in their emotion, like sadness, helps them journey through that emotional landscape with you by their side.

3. **Encouraging Dialogue:** Encourage your children to express their thoughts and feelings. You can ask open-ended questions at dinner or bedtime, such as "What was the best part of your day?" This regular communication between you and your children lets them know that you care about what's happening in their lives and that you are always someone they can talk to.

Modeling self-love and self-respect is the most powerful way to teach these qualities to your children. When children see their parents treating themselves with kindness and respect, they learn that these are important values. They are always watching and listening! They learn that self-care is not selfish but necessary to live a healthy, balanced life. Moreover, when they see their parents setting boundaries, they learn to set their own, understanding that they have the right to protect their emotional space. Parenting with self-love and compassion enhances your own life and profoundly influences your children, equipping them with the emotional skills and values that promote a healthy, fulfilling lives. As you continue to integrate these practices into your parenting approach, you will likely find that they make parenting more enjoyable and effective, creating a family environment rich in love, respect, and mutual understanding.

"Having children has been a huge part of my self-love journey. Children are your ultimate measuring stick. You might think you have things figured out, but they will reveal any area where you still need to grow. For me, that was with my anger. I had a lot of shame and hatred for myself when I would yell at my kids. It took a lot of self-compassion to start to overcome that. I was so ashamed of myself. But my kids look at me with so much love, even after I've not been a great mom. And that love is so powerful. If they can keep loving me, I know I can keep loving me."

Petra

Exercise: Better Communication with Your Children

- If you have children, think of ways to foster more communication with them. Could you be more present at dinner? Or take a walk with them in the evening as the sun sets? Schedule a one-on-one date? Think of some things you'd like to ask them that would better help you understand the world through their eyes.

CHAPTER 5:

Building Inner Strength and Resilience

Life is full of challenges. Yet, no matter what life brings our way, inner strength, resilience, and self-love form a robust framework for navigating challenges and fostering well-being despite failure, opposition, disappointment, or loss. Inner strength is the ability to draw upon our mental, emotional, and spiritual resources to persevere through difficult times. It involves resilience in the face of adversity, courage to confront challenges, and determination to stay true to our values and goals. Cultivating inner strength allows us to withstand setbacks, bounce back from failures, and face life's uncertainties more confidently and calmly.

Resilience is the capacity to adapt positively to stress, adversity, trauma, or significant sources of risk. It involves maintaining a stable equilibrium and recovering quickly from difficult experiences, whether at home, at work, or in our inner world. Resilience is not about avoiding stress or hardships but rather about tolerating unpleasant experiences and ultimately learning and growing from them. Developing coping strategies and maintaining a sense of hope and optimism despite setbacks enable us to navigate life's ups and downs with extraordinary grace and fortitude, fostering a sense of empowerment and greater self-love in our journey toward living a fulfilling and meaningful life.

"My love for myself is present through any challenge. I am resilient."

Resilience Training: Techniques for Tough Times

Resilience is the ability to be flexible and adjust to challenging life experiences. Whether these challenges emerge from everyday stressors or more significant life changes, the capacity to bounce back and thrive is invaluable. To endure difficult experiences, a strong relationship with ourselves is essential, along with various techniques that help ground us in the present moment and think positive, supportive thoughts. Research has found that we aren't born resilient but can cultivate resources and skills to develop this muscle. Resilience training encompasses methods and strategies that help make facing adversities with a steadier heart and clearer mind possible.

Grounding and mindfulness exercises are fundamental components of resilience training. These practices anchor you in the present moment, providing calm amid the storm of stress and anxiety. One effective grounding technique is the "5-4-3-2-1" exercise, a sensory awareness practice that can be done anywhere, anytime. Begin by taking a couple of deep, calming breaths. Then, look around and name five things you can see, four things you can touch, three things you can hear, two things you can smell, and one thing you can taste. This technique draws your focus away from sources of stress and centers your mind, reducing feelings of overwhelm and anxiety.

Mindfulness meditation, another resilience-building practice, involves sitting quietly and paying attention to thoughts, sounds, bodily sensations, and breathing—bringing your attention back to the present whenever your mind wanders. Regular mindfulness meditation enhances your ability to detach from negative thoughts and emotional reactions, providing a clearer perspective and facilitating a more measured response to stress. This mental discipline not only diminishes the impact of stress in the moment but also contributes to long-term emotional resilience, enhancing your ability to navigate life's ups and downs with greater ease and less distress.

Cognitive restructuring is another crucial aspect of resilience training. This cognitive behavioral therapy technique involves identifying and challenging negative thought patterns that can contribute to feelings of helplessness and despair. For instance, transforming thoughts like "I can never do anything right" into "I can learn from my mistakes and improve" shifts your mindset from defeat to growth and possibility. Systematically addressing and altering these harmful thought patterns enhances your resilience and overall mental health and well-being.

The development of a strong support network is integral to enhancing resilience. Social support provides emotional comfort and practical help in times of need. To cultivate and maintain a robust network, contact family, friends, and colleagues who understand and support your aspirations and values. Invest time in these relationships by offering support and actively engaging in shared activities. Additionally, consider joining groups or communities that align with your interests or experiences. These connections can provide diverse perspectives and solutions during challenging times, reinforcing your emotional resilience.

Building this network also involves learning to ask for help when needed, a skill that requires courage and humility but is essential for fostering resilience. Remember: Seeking support is not a sign of weakness but rather a strategic approach to overcoming obstacles. The more you engage with your support network, the more resources you will have when facing challenges. This network provides practical assistance and enhances your sense of belonging and purpose, which are crucial for long-term resilience and personal growth.

Through these resilience-building techniques—grounding exercises, mindfulness, cognitive restructuring, and the development of a support network—you equip yourself with a toolkit that helps you navigate challenging times and enriches your daily life. These practices strengthen your mental and emotional foundations, ensuring you are prepared to meet future challenges with confidence and poise. As you continue to incorporate these strategies into your routine, observe how they influence your reactions to stress and adversity, and take note of the increased ease with which you handle the trials of life. This ongoing practice is about coping and thriving, transforming each challenge into an opportunity for growth and learning.

"I actually gained so much self-love through my infertility battle. I have never really struggled with self-love, but the boost of realizing what a badass I truly am to weather such a storm was actually surprising to me. My infertility made me love myself so much more, which is completely contrary to how most feel. And then I just lost our second IVF baby at 22 weeks; another storm I braved and came through. We are planning to transfer our third and final baby boy embryo at the end of summer. Praying this little boy will give our first son a baby brother."

Erin

Exercise: Where Have You Been Resilient?

- Think back on a time in your life when you were resilient. What did you endure? What courage and strength did you conjure to overcome that challenge? And what lessons did you learn about life and yourself? Meditate or journal about this.

- Now, how does your perception of yourself change when you recall the strength and resilience you've had in the past? Take some time to reflect or journal.

Harnessing Personal Failures for Growth and Learning

In our culture, the notion of failure often carries a heavy weight, typically seen as an endpoint rather than a pivotal growth point to propel us to new heights. By shifting our perspective and treating failures as indispensable learning opportunities, we can extract value from them, turning apparent setbacks into setups for future success and amplifying our resilience. Building resilience is recognizing that the path to our hopes and dreams is paved with lessons learned from our mistakes.

Many are familiar with the story of Thomas Edison, whose endeavors to invent the electric light bulb were met with thousands of unsuccessful attempts. Each failure brought him closer to the solution, and each misstep gave him a clue about what might work instead. Edison famously said, "I have not failed. I've just found 10,000 ways that won't work." His persistence eventually led to a breakthrough that dramatically changed the world. Similarly, before becoming one of the most famous authors in the world, J.K. Rowling faced numerous rejections from publishers. Her perseverance despite these rejections was fueled by her belief in her book and her willingness to learn from each rejection until she finally found a publisher willing to take a chance on Harry Potter.

Learning from failures, however, involves more than just perseverance; it requires an inner strength to analyze what went wrong and what we could do better next time. One effective technique is performing a post-failure reflection, which includes documenting the details of the failure, identifying factors that contributed to the outcome, and formulating a plan for future attempts. This could involve modifying our strategy, stopping to acquire new skills, or adjusting goals to be more realistic.

Practicing self-love and compassion while navigating failure requires approaching this process without self-judgment, allowing yourself to see each failure as a step toward your dreams.

A shift in mindset can also significantly alter your relationship with failure. Viewing your actions and their outcomes as experiments helps dilute the fear of failing and support a spirit of innovation and creativity. After all, you're just experimenting! Each attempt, successful or not, is merely another opportunity to collect data, which is invaluable in guiding future decisions and strategies. This mindset encourages risk-taking and supports a dynamic learning environment where adaptability and flexibility lead to unexpected solutions and success.

By embracing failure as a natural part of the learning process, you empower yourself to take risks and push boundaries, knowing that each failure is not a reflection of your worth but a valuable lesson guiding you toward your dreams and goals. This approach enhances personal growth and achievement and builds resilience as you become more adept at navigating challenges and setbacks with confidence, self-compassion, and self-love. As you continue to learn from each experience, remember that the most profound successes come from the courage to fail and the wisdom to love ourselves enough to try again.

"When I was in my early twenties, I struggled with self-love a lot. I had so little of it that I would often hold my hand up in front of my face as if I was shielding myself from the sun, but really, I was just hiding from the world. I had so much shame and such low self-worth. But I also loved dancing, and it was one of the few places where I found myself loving that girl in the mirror. I was also really poor at that time, barely able to feed myself, and I had my eyes on a dance job that was one of the best-paying jobs in the city at that time. I went to the audition and totally bombed. I showed up in sweats while the other dancers had full make-up, colorful leotards, tan tights, and heels. I was determined to try again the next year. However, I was really ill, and despite my best attempts, I could not land the job. Another year rolled by, and I went back yet again to get that job. This time, I knew how to present myself and exactly what they wanted from me, and sure enough, I got the job. It was a turning point in my life and my self-worth increased tremendously. If I could do that, think of what else I could do! I also consistently made more money after that. I turned a corner in so many ways. Not that it was easy after that, but life was just different. I was playing the game of life at a new level. I knew I could accomplish things if I never gave up."

Natasha

Exercise: Where Can You Let Yourself Fail?

- Reflect on a failure in your past that opened a doorway you never would have expected. Perhaps a breakup that made way for your current partner? Or a job you got fired from that opened a new opportunity?

- When you reframe failure as growth and learning in those moments, what does that do to your relationship with yourself? Take some time to reflect and journal.

The Link Between Self-Love and Assertiveness

Assertiveness is often misunderstood as merely a communication style, yet it encompasses so much more, particularly in the realm of self-love. Assertive communication is a respectful and confident way of expressing thoughts, feelings, and needs while maintaining respect for oneself and others. It is a crucial form of self-respect and an essential component of self-love because it involves honoring your needs and boundaries. By being assertive, you advocate for yourself and ensure your voice is heard and considered, reinforcing your self-worth and self-esteem. This proactive stance is fundamental in personal scenarios and professional environments, where clear communication and boundary-setting are often necessary for healthy workplace dynamics.

Here are some examples of assertive communication:

1. **Setting boundaries:** "I appreciate your enthusiasm, but I need some alone time right now. I'm going to take some time to recharge."

2. **Expressing feelings:** "I felt hurt when you made that comment during the meeting. I'd like us to discuss how we can communicate better in the future."

3. **Making requests:** "Could you please let me know in advance next time you want to borrow my car? I didn't feel respected when you borrowed it without checking in with me."

4. **Giving constructive feedback:** "I think your idea has potential, but I have some concerns about its feasibility. How about we work together to address these issues?"

Assertive communication involves clearly stating thoughts or feelings, using "I" statements to take ownership of emotions, being specific about needs or preferences, and maintaining a respectful tone toward the other person. These allow you to express your feelings and thoughts without blaming or criticizing others. This approach helps to foster open and honest communication while respecting both parties' boundaries and feelings. Your feelings and boundaries deserve to be respected! As do others.

One common misconception is conflating assertiveness with aggression. Aggression disregards the needs, feelings, or opinions of others and often involves imposing one's own needs at the expense of others. Assertiveness, in contrast, maintains a balance. It respects your rights and those of others. For example, an aggressive person might demand, "You must listen to me!" whereas an assertive individual would say, "I would like to share my thoughts on this." This distinction is crucial because it highlights that assertiveness is built on respect—respect for oneself and others—making it a healthy interpersonal strategy that fosters understanding and collaboration.

Developing assertiveness can be transformative; like any skill, it requires practice and dedication. One skill many must practice to be assertive is saying "No." Practicing saying no is an integral part of being assertive. It involves understanding your limits and not overcommitting yourself, which is essential for maintaining self-love and well-being. Setting clear boundaries is equally important; it defines what you are comfortable with and how you expect to be treated by others. Boundaries can be related to your time, energy, or emotional availability, and communicating these can help prevent misunderstandings and resentment.

The benefits of assertiveness extend far beyond just improved communications. They directly impacts the quality of your relationships by fostering mutual respect and understanding. When you're assertive, you are more likely to attract and cultivate relationships with others who respect your boundaries and treat you well. Furthermore, assertiveness boosts self-confidence. Each time you successfully express your needs and have them acknowledged; it reinforces your belief in your value. This can be incredibly empowering, especially for those who have previously struggled with low self-esteem or passivity. Others often give you more respect when they see that you respect yourself enough to assert your needs and boundaries. This respect can enhance your professional and personal relationships, providing a foundation for healthier interactions.

Incorporating assertiveness into your daily life might initially feel challenging, especially if you are not accustomed to articulating your needs or have been conditioned to prioritize the needs of others above your own. However, the shift toward assertive communication can significantly enhance your relationship with yourself and others, leading to a more fulfilling and respectful engagement with the world around you. As you practice and become more comfortable asserting, you will insist that the world hear what you say and treat you the way you deserve to be treated. That is the embodiment of loving yourself! It also transforms your interactions and deepens your self-love practice, reinforcing the undeniable truth that you deserve respect and consideration. Your voice and boundaries matter!

"When I had very low self-love, I never said no to anyone. I just went along with everything anyone else wanted to do. When I look at my life now, with the self-love I currently have, I say no all the time. That's so interesting to me. Maybe that's why children so easily say no to what they don't want to do. They haven't had their assertiveness and self-love beaten out of them by the world yet. Self-love and assertiveness are their natural state. I'm so glad I got mine back after all those years without it!

Maribel

Exercise: Practicing Assertiveness

- Commit to being assertive at least once every day this week.

- Write out some examples of assertiveness you could practice this week. Find at least one for each category: Setting boundaries, expressing feelings, making a request, or giving constructive feedback.

- Next, write a few examples of things you could say "No" to.

- Now practice saying each phrase out loud so that you have practiced it in advance. New skills require practice!

Handling Criticism Without Losing Self-Worth

Navigating the waters of both constructive and destructive criticism can be daunting, yet it is an inevitable part of building inner strength and resilience. Understanding the nature of the feedback you receive is crucial in maintaining your self-worth and using criticism as a stepping stone to personal and professional growth rather than a stumbling block. Constructive criticism, often intended to foster growth, comes with an element of support and aims to improve specific aspects of your behavior or performance. It is generally specific, manageable, and delivered with respect. On the other hand, destructive criticism tends to be vague, infused with negativity, and often leaves you feeling demeaned rather than empowered.

To differentiate effectively between these two types of feedback, it's essential to consider the intent behind the words. Constructive feedback usually aligns with your goals and is presented as an opportunity for improvement. In contrast, destructive criticism does not offer a clear route for growth and may align with the critic's frustrations or biases. When faced with criticism, take a moment to assess the content and the context in which it is given. Ask yourself whether it provides specific guidance and is relevant to your objectives. This assessment can help you filter out unhelpful criticisms and focus on feedback that genuinely aims to support your development.

Equipping yourself with emotional coping strategies is essential when handling criticism. One practical approach is reframing, which involves changing your perspective on the feedback to view it as an opportunity for learning rather than a personal attack. For instance, if you receive criticism about a project at work, rather than dwelling on any negative emotion it evokes, try to identify key takeaways that could enhance your future work. Taking some deep breaths, going for a walk, or taking a break to eat something can also help you move through the emotion this brings up. Ultimately this shift in perspective will reduce the emotional weight of the criticism and help you focus on your growth and improvement.

Another helpful strategy is seeking second opinions. If you receive particularly hard-to-digest feedback, discussing it with trusted colleagues or friends can provide new insights and help you see the bigger picture. This helps validate the criticism and gives you a more rounded view of your abilities and areas for improvement. It's important to choose supportive and objective individuals for these discussions to ensure that you get constructive advice.

Assertive communication is critical in responding to unjust or destructive criticism. It involves expressing your feelings clearly and calmly without being passive or aggressive. For example, if a colleague makes an unfounded critique about your work ethic, you could respond with "I understand that you might see it differently, but I am committed to my work and continuously strive to perform at my best. Could you specify any particular instances that led to your observation?" This kind of response addresses the criticism directly, reinforces your self-respect, and sets boundaries regarding how you expect to be treated.

Fostering a growth mindset is another critical aspect of dealing with criticism. This mindset revolves around the belief that your abilities and intelligence can be developed over time through dedication and hard work. It encourages viewing challenges and failures as growth opportunities, which can make receiving criticism a less daunting experience. When you adopt a growth mindset, you are more likely to actively engage with constructive feedback and use it to foster personal and professional development. Some examples of a growth mindset are:

1. **Embracing challenges:** Instead of avoiding difficult tasks, someone with a growth mindset actively seeks out challenges as opportunities to learn and improve. For example, they might take on a new work project requiring them to learn new skills.

2. **Learning from criticism:** Instead of feeling discouraged by feedback or criticism, someone with a growth mindset sees it as constructive input for growth. They might ask for specific examples and use the feedback to make improvements.

3. **Persisting in the face of setbacks:** Rather than giving up when faced with obstacles or failures, a person with a growth mindset persists and tries alternative strategies. For instance, if they fail to achieve a goal, they reflect on what went wrong and adjust their approach accordingly.

4. **Seeking inspiration and learning from others:** Someone with a growth mindset admires and learns from the success of others. They view successful people not as threats but as sources of inspiration and motivation to improve themselves.

5. **Believing in effort and perseverance:** Instead of believing that success is solely based on innate talent, a person with a growth mindset believes that effort and perseverance are critical factors in achieving their goals. They understand that mastery takes time and dedication.

6. **Celebrating progress and milestones:** Rather than solely focusing on the end result, someone with a growth mindset celebrates the progress they make along the way. They recognize that every step forward, no matter how small, contributes to their overall growth and development.

These examples demonstrate how individuals with a growth mindset approach challenges, feedback, setbacks, and learning opportunities with a positive and proactive attitude, ultimately fostering continuous improvement and personal development.

You can handle criticism without undermining your self-worth by understanding the types of criticism, adopting emotional coping strategies, practicing assertive communication, and fostering a growth mindset. These skills help maintain your confidence and self-respect and turn potentially negative experiences into opportunities for personal growth and success. As you navigate the complexities of receiving and processing feedback, remember that your response to criticism often defines your path to personal growth and resilience. Can you love yourself through criticism? Yes, you can!

"I have a very critical mother, which has made me very sensitive to other people's energy. I need a lot of alone time and space. I still have a lot of work to do to learn how to receive other people's input without getting anxious and getting in my head. I need better boundaries. I think I let the criticism or other people's ideas in as if they were my own. It has created a lot of health challenges for me. But I'm really working to overcome that now. I have a new baby who's very sensitive, too. So, I think he is forcing me to work on this for both our sakes!"

Jena

Exercise: What is Your Growth Mindset?

- Take a criticism you have received in your life, either constructive or destructive, and apply a growth mindset to it. How could you view that challenge or failure as an opportunity for growth? Take some time to reflect and journal.

Work-Life Balance and Overcoming Imposter Syndrome

Work-Life Balance

Cultivating resilience means cultivating work-life balance. In today's fast-paced world, it's easy to find oneself wearing the mask of a professional role long after the workday ends. This blurring of lines between who we are in our professional lives and who we are outside of them can lead to a loss of personal identity and, inevitably, significant stress. The challenge often lies in the intense demands of modern work cultures that value overwork and undervalue personal time. The result can be a feeling that you're never quite meeting expectations in any areas of your life, constantly juggling and often dropping the ball somewhere. This can lead to burnout—emotional, physical, and mental exhaustion caused by prolonged stress.

Maintaining work-life balance involves setting clear boundaries for when and where you engage in work-related activities, for example, making a rule not to check work emails or take calls during family meals. Similarly, having a dedicated workspace that you can physically step away from can help mentally distancing yourself from work tasks, signaling to your brain that it's time to focus on your personal life. Another effective strategy is engaging in mindfulness practices, which can enhance your ability to switch between professional and personal modes. Techniques such as meditation or focused breathing exercises can help clear your mind of work-related thoughts and center your attention on your personal life during non-work hours. These practices improve your ability to compartmentalize and reduce stress, enhancing overall life satisfaction.

Setting realistic boundaries in your professional life is critical to maintaining this balance. This means learning to say no to additional responsibilities when your workload is substantial or to the tasks do not align with your professional goals or personal values. It's important to communicate these boundaries clearly and assertively, ensuring that colleagues and superiors understand your limits and respect them. This might involve negotiating deadlines or delegating tasks to others. Remember, setting boundaries is not a sign of incapacity or unwillingness but a necessary measure for maintaining your health and ensuring you remain productive and engaged long-term.

Beyond managing your professional identity, it's equally vital to cultivate a rewarding personal life that reflects your interests and passions. Engaging in hobbies and activities outside work can significantly enhance your quality of life and sense of self-worth. Whether it's painting, hiking, reading, or volunteering, these activities provide a counterbalance to work, offering personal fulfillment that professional accomplishments might not. They remind you that your value extends beyond your professional output, encompassing your creativity, kindness, curiosity, and other personal traits.

Fostering this balanced identity safeguards your well-being and potentially enhances your professional performance. By not allowing work to consume all your energy and time, you can bring a fresher perspective and renewed vigor to your professional roles. Likewise, by enriching your personal life with diverse interests and activities, you ensure that your self-esteem and satisfaction are not wholly contingent on your professional success, which can fluctuate. This holistic approach to identity management enhances your quality of life and makes you a more balanced, contented, and ultimately prosperous woman.

Overcoming Imposter Syndrome

Have you ever felt like a fraud, secretly fearing you might be exposed for not being as competent or intelligent as others believe? This phenomenon is known as imposter syndrome, a psychological pattern where individuals doubt their accomplishments and have a persistent, often internalized fear of being exposed as a fraud. It usually surfaces in moments of new job roles, promotion, public recognition, or when comparing oneself to peers who seem more knowledgeable or capable. These situations share a common theme: They place individuals in positions where their abilities are on display, scrutinized, and potentially compared to others. Despite external evidence of their competence, those experiencing this syndrome remain convinced that they are frauds who do not deserve the success they have achieved. This can lead to significant anxiety and stress, particularly in professional environments or in situations where their skills and contributions are recognized.

To combat imposter syndrome, start with reframing your thoughts. Cognitive restructuring is a powerful tool that involves identifying negative thought patterns and challenging their validity. For instance, if you find yourself thinking "I don't know what I'm doing," counter that thought with evidence of your past successes and the skills you employed to achieve them. This helps in grounding your self-perception in reality rather than fear. Discussing your feelings with trusted peers or mentors can also be incredibly beneficial. Often, you'll find that others have experienced similar feelings of inadequacy, which normalizes the experience and can diminish its power over you.

Moreover, vocalizing your thoughts can provide new perspectives, reinforcing your legitimate right to achievements. Lastly, maintaining a success journal is another effective strategy. Regularly document your accomplishments, the challenges you overcame, the skills you applied, and the compliments you received. This record is a tangible reminder of your capabilities and successes, boosting your confidence whenever doubts creep in.

Self-compassion is a vital ally in dealing with imposter syndrome. It encourages an attitude of kindness and understanding toward oneself rather than harsh self-judgment. When you recognize and accept that perfection is unattainable and that all humans are fallible, you begin to view your mistakes and shortcomings with more sympathy and less judgment. Practicing self-compassion involves treating yourself with the same kindness, concern, and support that you would offer to a good friend.

A practical exercise in self-compassion is the Self-Compassion Pause. Take a moment to pause whenever you notice self-critical thoughts, especially those fueling imposter syndrome. Place your hand over your heart, feel its beat, breathe deeply, and speak kindly to yourself. Acknowledge the challenge you are facing with phrases like, "This is a tough moment for me," followed by messages of support: "I am capable and have overcome similar challenges before." This practice not only soothes your immediate anxiety but also gradually alters your internal dialogue to be more supportive and less critical. Overcoming imposter syndrome is not about never feeling doubts but managing them effectively so they no longer hinder your growth or diminish your achievements. Through these efforts, you reinforce your inner strength and resilience, weaving those vibrant threads more prominently into the tapestry of your life.

"Something really clicked into place for me when I realized that self-love flows much more freely to me when there is enough TIME. Somehow, time seems to be a factor in many aspects of self-love for me, and when I slow down the pace of my life and live more consciously, I don't end up blaming myself for things to the same degree. There is time to breathe, to sense, to do the things I like to do and that are good for me, to do things properly, to help others... Basically, when there is enough time, it is easier to be the person I want to be; the self-blame and resentment go quiet, and self-love can flow."

Renee

Exercise: Self-Compassion Pause

- Take a moment and practice a Self-Compassion Pause. Place your hand over your heart, feel its beat, breathe deeply, and speak kindly to yourself. Some examples are: "You're doing such a great job pushing ahead," "I'm so proud of your hard work," or "Even though it's difficult, you're doing it! Just one step at a time."

- Acknowledge the challenge you face with compassion, followed by messages of support, encouragement, and self-love such as "It's painful for me to be feeling this right now but I know I'm safe," or "This is a big project I took on, but I can do it."

- You can use this technique whenever you are overwhelmed by negative emotions, acknowledging your pain or stress and offering comfort.

CHAPTER 6:

Advanced Self-Love Techniques

Advanced self-love goes beyond basic self-care practices and involves a deep, intentional, and ongoing commitment to nurturing one's own well-being, growth, and happiness. When self-love overflows, it's a spiritual experience that involves a deep knowing of our worthiness, radical acceptance of ourselves and our lives, and a deep compassion for oneself that is calming and peaceful. That spiritual love expands out into the physical world into the life we live, our careers, our finances, and our communities. Advancing our self-love means expanding beyond just loving ourselves through self-care and healthy boundaries, and stepping into a world where abundance flows, our relationships flourish, and the world around us, our home and community, reflect this level of love.

"My love for myself is reflected back in my work, finances, relationships, and community."

The Intersection of Spirituality and Self-Love

In the vast landscape of self-love, spirituality often emerges as a profound source of renewal and connection, offering pathways that lead to greater personal harmony and a more profound acceptance of oneself. Spirituality, irrespective of the specific practices or beliefs it encompasses, fundamentally seeks to connect us with something greater than ourselves—be it the divine, the universe, or our inner essence. This connection fosters a sense of belonging and peace, integral to loving and valuing oneself profoundly.

Exploring the myriad ways spiritual practices can enhance self-love, it's essential to consider how these practices encourage us to look beyond the superficial aspects of our lives and touch upon the deeper truths of our existence. Prayer, meditation, and various spiritual rituals allow us to step out of the daily hustle and into a quiet introspection and peaceful space. For instance, meditation offers a way to calm the mind and foster awareness and presence, which are essential for recognizing our worth and beauty. Similarly, prayer can provide comfort and reassurance, reminding us of our connection to a more significant power.

Spiritual rituals, varying widely among different cultures and religions, often ground us in our values and remind us of our profound connection with the world around us. These rituals, whether lighting candles, chanting, or other acts of devotion, help align our actions with our beliefs and intentions. Engaging in these practices can be particularly powerful in reinforcing a state of self-compassion and acceptance, as they often emphasize the qualities of forgiveness, gratitude, and unconditional love—key components of self-love.

Being part of a spiritual community can significantly enrich these experiences, providing a nurturing environment where you can explore your spirituality alongside others on similar paths. These communities offer not only companionship but also opportunities for learning and growth. Within such groups, you can find mentors and peers who can provide guidance, support, and valuable perspectives to help you navigate your spiritual and self-love journey. The sense of belonging and acceptance in these communities can be incredibly affirming, reinforcing your self-worth and helping you feel valued and understood.

Moreover, spiritual communities often engage in activities that promote service and altruism, further enhancing feelings of self-love. Helping others and contributing to a community can boost your self-esteem and provide a sense of purpose and fulfillment. These activities remind us of our ability to make a positive impact, reinforcing our sense of agency and self-worth.

The goal of integrating spirituality into your self-love practice is not to conform to a specific doctrine or set of rules but to discover personal meaning and connection that enhances your sense of self-worth and enrich your life. Whether through quiet reflection, active participation in community rituals, or private expressions of faith, embracing your spirituality can be a powerful component of your self-love practice. As you continue to explore and integrate these spiritual dimensions, they will bring comfort, connection, and a profound depth to your understanding and practice of self-love.

"I'm in a group that meets regularly, and we all have started meditating. I realized that it was because I was doing meditation every day that I gradually got to a place where I loved myself completely, and I loved everybody else, too. So, I think I just need to keep doing my spiritual practice because that's what's giving me the ability to really love myself. And I think that's true of everyone I talk to, that any kind of meditation does that, and everybody agrees, we're all in a good place for doing this for so long."

Jacqueline

Exercise: Exploring Personal Spirituality

- Start by closing your eyes and reflecting on what spirituality means to you and how it relates to your feelings of self-worth and love. Who are you? The part of you that is not your body. Who is observing you asking that question? When everything goes quiet inside of you, what do you find there?

Harnessing the Power of Visualization for Self-Acceptance

Visualization is a remarkably potent tool that can transform your self-image and enhance self-acceptance. At its core, visualization involves creating vivid and detailed mental images of situations you desire to manifest in your life, including seeing yourself as a person filled with self-love and acceptance. This technique leverages the brain's remarkable ability to interpret imagery as equivalent to real-life action, thereby influencing your emotions and behaviors toward achieving those visualized outcomes.

Visualization is not mere daydreaming; it is an active, intentional practice that engages the subconscious mind, tapping into its potential to reshape thoughts and behaviors. For instance, by consistently visualizing yourself speaking confidently in public or approaching personal challenges calmly, you begin to forge new cognitive pathways that reinforce these behaviors in real situations. The mental rehearsal provided by visualization primes you to act in ways that align with the images you've cultivated, thus fostering a more positive self-image and greater self-acceptance.

The benefits of visualization are supported by various psychological studies and neuroscientific research. These studies[6] show that the brain often does not distinguish between real and vividly imagined experiences. Because of this, the emotions and endorphins produced during visualization can be as influential as those triggered by actual events. For example, athletes often use visualization to improve performance, mentally rehearsing their sport to enhance their physical prowess. Similarly, visualization can enhance feelings of self-worth

---

6   Dijkstra, N., Fleming, S.M. Subjective signal strength distinguishes reality from imagination. *Nat Commun* **14**, 1627 (2023). https://doi.org/10.1038/s41467-023-37322-1

and acceptance, effectively training your brain to focus on positive self-regard and to reject negative self-judgments.

Visualization can also lead to significant changes in behavior. By frequently visualizing yourself acting in ways that reflect self-compassion and self-acceptance, you shift your behavior patterns in reality. This shift can lead to more profound changes in how you view yourself and interact with others, ultimately fostering a more loving and accepting self-relationship. But why stop there? In addition to visualizing yourself acting in ways that are compassionate and loving toward yourself, why not visualize the kind of life you'd be living if you loved yourself that much? How much money would you make if you loved yourself more? Where would you live? What kind of projects would you be working on? Who would your friends be?

Regularly engaging in visualization allows you to experience a reality where self-love and acceptance are fully realized. Even just a few minutes each day spent visualizing positive interactions and success can effectively influence your self-perception and actions throughout the day. Consider integrating visualization into your morning routine to set a positive tone for the day or use it to unwind in the evening, reflecting on and reinforcing the day's successes. This practice enhances your emotional resilience and empowers you to bring about the changes in your life that align with your deepest values and aspirations. As you continue to harness the power of visualization, it becomes a vital tool in your toolkit.

"One very loving thing I've done for myself is that no matter what I've been through and all the disappointments in my love life, I just kept visualizing myself having what I wanted. And finally, over a couple of years, it all came true. I became the woman who could receive and have that love."

Lisa

Exercise: Visualize Your Way to Self-Love

- Close your eyes and take a few deep breaths to relax your body and clear your mind.

- Imagine a scene in which you embody a trait or achieve a goal representing your ideal self-love and acceptance. Make the scene as detailed as possible—incorporate what you are wearing, who you might be with, what the setting is, and most importantly, how you feel in that moment. Try to invoke all your senses to make the experience feel as real as possible.

- The emotional component of this practice is crucial; try to genuinely feel the joy, confidence, or peace that comes with the scene you are visualizing. This emotional engagement can profoundly impact your mood and outlook, positively reinforcing your self-image.

Integrating Self-Love into Career Development

Align Career Goals with Personal Values

One of the most empowering steps you can take in your career is ensuring that your professional goals and tasks align with your personal values and definitions of success. This alignment is crucial because when your work resonates with what you hold dear, it brings a sense of purpose and satisfaction that transcends monetary compensation. Begin this alignment by reflecting on what values are most important to you—be it creativity, service, innovation, or leadership. Ask yourself how these values can be integrated into your current job role or how they might guide you toward a new career path that feels more congruent with your true self.

For instance, if you value social impact, you might seek roles that allow you to contribute to projects that benefit the community or the environment. Alternatively, if creativity is your cornerstone, consider injecting creativity into your daily tasks or pivoting toward a role that inherently calls for creative thinking, such as marketing, design, or content creation. Aligning your career with your values enhances job satisfaction and builds a professional identity that mirrors your true self, fostering a more profound sense of self-love and respect.

Seek Fulfilling Roles

While financial compensation is essential, finding joy and fulfillment in your daily work is equally vital for maintaining self-love. Seek out roles that challenge you, grow your skills, and excite you about showing up daily. If your current role feels lacking, consider how you could reshape it. Could you propose a new project that aligns more closely with your interests? Is there a training course that could expand your capabilities and lead to more engaging work?

If changing your role within your current job isn't possible, it may be time to look for new opportunities that will offer a better fit. Network within your industry to learn about different roles, or consider speaking with a career coach who can provide guidance based on your skills and passions. You deserve a fulfilling career!

Advocate for Yourself

Advocating for yourself in the workplace is a powerful form of self-love. It involves speaking up for your needs, whether negotiating salary, requesting resources necessary for your work, or seeking opportunities for advancement. Self-advocacy requires confidence and a strong sense of worth—a direct reflection of self-love.

Prepare for negotiations by thoroughly researching average salaries and benefits in your field so you can present informed requests. Approach conversations with management confidently, expressing your value to the company clearly and professionally. Remember, advocating for yourself affects your current position and salary and sets a precedent for how you are treated professionally. It's about respecting and valuing your contribution, reinforcing your self-love and self-respect.

"It happened about seven years ago after rebuilding myself after a burnout. I deeply followed the impulse that told me to reconnect with professional dance, my first profession. That day, I entered a huge, bright dance studio of a large, famous European ballet company... More than 70 dancers were waiting to do their barre, and I was introduced to the whole company by one of the Ballet Masters as an emotional therapist. I was welcomed and applauded very warmly. Waiting for all to begin to work together, I felt an immense happiness to have listened to myself and a great serenity to be in my right place."

Aloysia

Exercise: Workplace Self-Advocacy

- Create a list of areas in your professional life where additional support or change could enhance your effectiveness and satisfaction.

- Write down potential solutions or requests for each item that could address these issues.

- Practice how you would present these ideas to your supervisor or team, focusing on how the changes will benefit not just you personally but the organization as a whole.

- This exercise will prepare you to advocate for yourself more effectively, enhancing your professional development and journey toward deeper self-love.

Financial Self-Care: Budgeting with Love

In today's world, the conventional metrics of financial success often revolve around accumulation—how much one can earn, own, or spend. However, true financial success extends beyond mere accumulation to encompass peace and security, nurturing a sense of well-being that resonates with your values and lifestyle choices. This approach to financial management, which I like to call "budgeting with love," prioritizes expenditures that enhance your life quality, align with your personal values, and contribute to your long-term happiness.

By redefining financial success, you are taking control of your financial destiny. It's a shift from viewing money as an end goal to seeing it as a means to support a fulfilling life. Consider what truly brings you happiness and contentment. Is it the security of savings, the experiences gained through travel, or perhaps the joy of learning new skills? By identifying these values, you can tailor your financial goals to support activities and services that enrich your life rather than mindlessly accumulating assets. This might mean allocating funds for a course in a subject you love, investing in health and wellness, or saving for future travel that expands your horizons and enriches your experience of the world.

Mindful spending is a critical practice in this approach. It involves making purchasing decisions that are consciously aligned with your long-term values and goals rather than impulsive buys that offer momentary satisfaction. To practice mindful spending, begin by observing your current spending habits without judgment. Track where your money goes for a month and notice which expenditures feel truly rewarding and which do not. This awareness allows you to make more informed choices, directing your money toward expenses that genuinely add value to your life.

For instance, buying a daily coffee might seem like a small indulgence, but if enjoying it significantly enhances your morning routine, it aligns well with the value of savoring small pleasures. Conversely, impulsively purchasing trendy clothing that doesn't fit your style or needs does not contribute to long-term satisfaction and those funds might be better redirected toward more fulfilling expenditures. This alignment of spending with your personal values brings a sense of satisfaction and contentment.

Developing a budget that accommodates self-care is crucial in this process. It's a way of showing yourself you are valued and cared for. Start by defining what self-care means to you—regular massage, psychological therapy, educational courses, or hobbies—and allocate a portion of your budget to these areas. This might require adjusting other spending areas, but the investment in your well-being always yields high returns. For example, dedicating funds to yoga classes or meditation workshops can significantly improve your mental and physical health, leading to greater happiness and productivity.

Lastly, the importance of investing in self-development cannot be overstated. Whether it's professional training to advance your career or personal development workshops that enhance your life skills, these investments contribute to your growth and well-being. They improve your competence and self-confidence and open up new opportunities for income and fulfillment. When budgeting for self-development, consider various resources, including books, online courses, retreats, or coaching sessions. These can offer valuable insights and skills that foster personal and professional growth.

Integrating these financial practices into your life creates a budget that reflects and supports your deepest values and aspirations. This approach ensures financial health and enriches your life, making each financial decision reflect your commitment to self-love and personal fulfillment. By managing your finances in this way, you cultivate a life that is not only financially secure, but also deeply rewarding.

"I find that the more I do things to make myself happy the more money I make. The better I take care of myself, the more my bank account reflects that."

Nikki

Exercise: What Does Financial Success Look Like for You?

- Take a few minutes to reflect on or journal what truly brings you happiness and contentment regarding finances. Is it the security of savings, the experiences gained through travel, or perhaps the joy of learning new skills? Does financial success mean owning more properties? More stocks? Or visit more countries with your partner or family?

- If your budget does not allocate money to your definition of financial success, make those changes today to align your finances with your vision for your future.

Community Involvement as an Expression of Self-Love

Community involvement is a powerful avenue for nurturing self-love as it fosters a profound sense of belonging and purpose. When you engage with your community by contributing your time, skills, or resources, you enrich the social fabric and deepen your connection to your surroundings and the people within it. This engagement often leads to a reinforced sense of self-worth and a more profound appreciation for your unique role in the tapestry of your community.

Participating in community activities allows you to step beyond your boundaries and immerse yourself in your neighborhood's or city's collective energy and aspirations. Volunteering at local organizations, for instance, can be a fulfilling way to give back, like mentoring youth, assisting at a local food bank, or contributing to community beautification projects. Engaging in community art projects can be particularly enriching. Painting murals, participating in community theater, or beautifying public spaces are just some of the creative outlets that can be therapeutic, enabling you to build a sense of accomplishment and pride in your contributions.

Giving back has a unique way of reinforcing one's sense of worth and purpose. When you contribute to the welfare of others, you receive profound emotional rewards—the feelings of gratitude and respect from those you help can significantly bolster your self-image. This reciprocal relationship between giving and receiving adds a rich layer of meaning to your life, affirming that you have valuable contributions to make. It also shifts your focus from inward reflection to outward contribution, which can be particularly beneficial if you are demanding of yourself. The appreciation you receive from community involvement reminds you of your worth and capabilities, countering negative self-perceptions and fostering a healthier, more loving self-view.

Networking locally is another aspect of community involvement that can significantly enhance your personal and professional life. Building relationships with like-minded individuals in your area can lead to new opportunities for collaboration and support. These connections provide emotional support, advice, and friendship, which are essential for personal growth and well-being. To cultivate such connections, you might attend local meetups, join clubs or groups related to your interests, or participate in community forums or workshops. These gatherings provide platforms for sharing ideas and resources, increasing your engagement with the community, and deepening your sense of belonging.

The impact of these activities extends beyond the immediate benefits of social interaction and emotional support; they also contribute to a strengthened community identity and resilience. Participating in and promoting community activities helps build a network of support and cooperation that can withstand and overcome challenges. This not only enhances your own life but also makes your community a better place to live for everyone. In this way, community involvement becomes a profound expression of self-love—you affirm your value and capabilities and contribute to a cycle of mutual support and appreciation that uplifts the entire community.

"Service to others has also been integral to my spiritual path. Helping others increases my love for them and increases my love for myself. At age 77, I am on a powerful spiritual path and experiencing unconditional love for myself and others."

Nancy

Exercise: Get Involved

- Do some research and find out how you can get more connected to your community. How can you share the love you have for yourself with others? How can you create a more loving community? In what way can you share your unique skillset and gifts?

- Send some emails, make some calls, and schedule some community involvement!

CHAPTER 7

Living a Life Anchored in Self-Love

Life is a journey of unknowns. None of us can predict the future or avoid the challenges ahead, but we can live a life anchored in such deep self-love that no matter what comes our way, we continue being loving and compassionate with ourselves. Life's challenges are not without sorrow, but we are not without resilience. Challenges invite learning more about life, uncovering new truths, and evolving on a personal and collective path in new directions. A life anchored in self-love is a commitment to never stopping learning, no matter how old, practicing gratitude, no matter how challenging the circumstances, and celebrating even the smallest victories along the way as a celebration of our unique and wonderful life. Self-love is a commitment to ourselves that nothing can shake. We deserve that lifetime of love.

"I'm committed to loving myself for the rest of my life."

Lifelong Learning as a Form of Self-Love

Lifelong learning is a deliberate and continuous effort to acquire new knowledge, skills, or understanding. As we age, it may seem that we already know everything. But a commitment to lifelong learning keeps our minds open to new possibilities, boosts our skills and self-confidence, and opens new opportunities for personal and professional growth. We don't know what we don't know, so continuous learning and a mindset that values growth, adaptability, and curiosity keep us open to new perspectives, relationships, joys and passions, and ways of loving ourselves. Lifelong learning is an essential component of a fulfilling life.

Engaging regularly in learning activities keeps your mind engaged and active. In a three-month study at the University of California, Riverside, researchers provided three classes weekly, two hours long, for a group of older adults, aged 58 to 86. Course options included singing, drawing, photography, Spanish, music composition, and education about what prevents successful aging. Not only did the participants significantly improve their cognitive scores for memory and attention, but in a follow-up study one year later, their cognitive abilities were similar to those of adults 50 years younger! The researchers were stunned that their cognitive scores continued to climb after the program's end, and they could only conclude that the encouragement to engage in continually learning and practicing new daily skills gave these older adults the memory and attention levels of college students.

Lifelong learning delays the effects of aging on the brain and boosts self-confidence. Each new skill mastered or subject understood reinforces your belief in your capabilities, fostering a resilient sense of self-worth immune to external validation. Continuous learning also opens doors to new opportunities, like keeping you relevant in your professional field. Beyond professional benefits, learning new skills can lead to unexpected passions and hobbies that enrich your life. For example, taking a course in photography might not only develop that skill but could also ignite a passion for visual storytelling, leading to new personal projects and even a side business.

Those who achieve higher levels of education age more slowly and live longer lives, according to a 2024 Columbia University study. Self-study is another valuable lifelong learning method, and it is as simple as reading books, watching educational videos, or listening to podcasts. What makes self-study effective is having clear goals and engaging with the material regularly. For example, if you want to improve your knowledge of history, you might set a goal to read one history book per month and watch a related documentary. This structured approach ensures that your self-study is consistent and provides health benefits.

Engaging in New Interests

Exploring new hobbies and interests is enjoyable and a powerful form of self-love, allowing you to break from your routine and learn more about your preferences and capabilities. Whether learning a new language, starting a craft, or exploring a new sport, each activity provides opportunities to challenge yourself, meet new people, and gain new experiences. Often, these activities lead to unexpected discoveries about yourself. You might find, for instance, that you have a talent for painting or a passion for rock climbing. These discoveries can be incredibly fulfilling, adding richness and excitement to your life.

Engaging in new hobbies as we age often helps us meet a community of like-minded individuals. Joining clubs or online communities related to your latest interest provides support and encouragement and deepens your engagement through shared experiences and discussions. For example, joining a local hiking club can enhance your enjoyment of the hobby through group hikes and shared tips on the best local trails. Joining a book club or spiritual group exposes you to other people's views on similar topics, challenging your ways of viewing the world and sharpening your mind.

Lifelong learning is more than just an educational pursuit; it is a lifestyle choice that nurtures your intellectual curiosity, bolsters self-esteem, and enriches life experience. Each learning opportunity is a step toward becoming a more well-rounded, knowledgeable, and confident version of yourself. This perspective shifts learning from a task or a goal to an integral part of your self-care routine, a true expression of self-love. By continually engaging in new learning experiences, you affirm your commitment to yourself, your growth, and your health, ensuring you remain open, adaptable, and vibrant at every stage. As you continue to explore new areas of knowledge and interest, it is a testament to your dedication to personal growth and self-love—a commitment that will lead to a more prosperous, more fulfilling life.

"After starting burlesque classes, joining a group, and starting to perform burlesque regularly, I had a profound shift in my self-love. Being part of a community that celebrates diversity on so many levels, plus the high of creating acts and performing them on stage, changed my life and my relationship with myself forever! And it turns out, I just love designing and making my own costumes!"

Cameron

Exercise: Find Your Next Learning Opportunity

- Take some time to look for a book, documentary, podcast series, or online class that sparks your interest. Commit to loving yourself through learning. You're doing this as you read this book!

- Now, make a list of subjects you'd like to study, courses you'd like to check out, or books that spark your interest. Commit to loving yourself through learning.

How to Love Ourselves Through Suffering or Tragedy

While much of our self-love journey improves our lives and relationships, suffering and sometimes even tragedy are unavoidable experiences in this life. Loving ourselves through suffering or tragedy can be an anchor through any storm, beginning with acknowledging our worthiness of love and compassion, and our resilience in the face of adversity. When confronted with challenges, whether personal loss, illness, or emotional turmoil, we often experience a range of emotions—from grief and despair to rage and confusion. These painful experiences can lead us to question the meaning of life, the existence of God, and if we feel responsible for what has occurred, a challenge to any self-love we've cultivated, as we grapple with self-blame, shame, or what feels like unforgivable regret. Amid these intense feelings or painful suffering, self-love starts with self-compassion. Self-compassion understands that suffering is a universal human experience and that we are not alone in our pain or choices.

In times of tragedy, though it may seem impossible, loving ourselves involves nurturing a sense of forgiveness and acceptance, forgiveness not just toward the situation or others involved, but, crucially, toward ourselves. We may grapple with guilt or self-blame, questioning decisions made or actions taken, which can devastate our self-love. However, self-love, always present beneath the surface, gently encourages us to acknowledge our imperfections and embrace self-compassion, regardless of what has come to pass. We can offer ourselves the same kindness and understanding we readily extend to others in similar circumstances. This practice of self-compassion and self-forgiveness is pivotal in rebuilding our emotional resilience and reaffirming our intrinsic value when self-love takes a hit.

Loving ourselves through suffering often requires seeking and accepting support from others. It's essential to recognize that vulnerability, or sharing our weaknesses, failures, or darkness with another, is not a weakness but a gateway to deeper connections and empathy. Those we share our pain with, be it trusted friends, family, or a therapist, can offer solace and perspective. This act reminds us that we are not alone in our struggles or the sometimes-unimaginable pain of life. In these moments, self-love is about honoring our need for connection and community while we endure life's most difficult losses. It's about understanding that reaching out to others is a testament to our strength, courage, and worthiness of love and comfort.

Loving ourselves through suffering or tragedy is nothing anyone looks forward to doing. But when faced with life's losses or suffering, our ability to continue to love ourselves and show up for what life is teaching us or transforming in us is a testament to our capacity for growth and transformation. Rooted in self-love, we can cultivate acceptance of what is, even when it makes no sense, isn't fair, or is cruel. We can also discover renewed gratitude for what we have, which may be the simplest pleasures. We can learn hard lessons about ourselves and find meaning in our experiences. While suffering may shape us, it does not define us. Through self-love, we reclaim our agency and power in the face of everything that is out of our control, in the face of our powerlessness, and we foster a more profound sense of compassion and understanding toward ourselves and others on our shared journey through life's trials.

"As an adoptee, I was primed basically in the womb and right after to spend my life on this journey of self-love. I'm not sure who thought telling an adoptee 'She [the birthmother] loved you so much, she gave you away,' would in any way teach an impressionable, lost, rejected child a path to self-love. Or did it? Because it was at that moment that I learned to fend for myself. I was the ONLY person who was going to love me because I believed everyone else thought I was discardable. When my children were very young, I used to stand them in front of the mirror and tell them 'See that guy? That guy will not let you down. He can't because he loves you and is your best friend.' I'd like to think that gave them the strength to persevere through bullies and just plain mean-spirited people. People who feel so small and entitled, they want to drag you down with them. Instead, I hoped my boys would have a deep sense of loving themselves because they knew that the guy in the mirror loved them. Self-love is sometimes the only thing we have in this world, and it is, by far, the most important. We can't fix anyone else, but we can love ourselves ANY TIME. Love, self-love, is always available."

Agnes

Exercise: Self-Compassion Practices for Survivors

- Take some time to cultivate self-compassion and write a compassionate letter to yourself. In this letter, address yourself like a dear friend who has experienced similar pain. Express understanding and care for the suffering you endured, affirm your worth and encourage yourself with compassion and hope.

- Read it out loud to yourself when you've finished.

- Notice how it feels in your body to receive that compassion from yourself.

Gratitude: Celebrating Small Victories in Everyday Life

No matter what happens in our daily lives, celebrating small victories is an act of gratitude and self-love. In pursuing self-growth and personal development, it's easy to become fixated on significant milestones—buying a house, graduating from school, or completing a long-term project. While these are worth celebrating, there is immense value in recognizing and celebrating the smaller achievements that occur in our daily lives. These small victories might seem inconsequential when viewed alone, but they are the steppingstones to our larger goals when added up. Celebrating them anchors us in a life of gratitude and self-appreciation while we take those steps toward our larger goals.

Every day, you likely accomplish tasks and progress in ways you might not even recognize as victories. Did you choose a healthy lunch when you could have indulged in fast food? Have you completed a daily exercise routine or taken a quick walk outdoors? You may have managed to meditate for ten minutes without distraction. Each action represents a small victory—a step toward a healthier, more balanced life. Celebrating these can drastically enhance your motivation to do more like this for yourself. For instance, treating yourself to a small reward after a week of healthy eating or acknowledging your consistency in exercise with a relaxing epsom salt bath can reinforce positive behaviors that you are doing for yourself. These celebrations need not be extravagant; the simplest acknowledgments are often the most effective.

Setting manageable, incremental goals is crucial in creating frequent opportunities for small victories. By breaking down a significant goal into smaller, more achievable objectives, you set yourself up for a series of successes. Each completed step boosts confidence and a sense of progress, which can be especially motivating when the end goal seems distant. For instance, if your goal is to write a book, setting a daily word count goal makes the process more manageable and allows you to celebrate small wins regularly.

This approach maintains your momentum and reduces the overwhelming feeling of pursuing big goals. The cumulative effect of these small successes is substantial.

Each small victory builds upon the last, creating more momentum and establishing a pattern of consistent achievement that amplifies your confidence and reinforces your commitment to your goals. Over time, what once seemed like a minor accomplishment becomes a critical component of a larger success story. This is the power of persistence and consistency, driven by celebrating and recognizing small victories.

Ultimately, a life celebrating small victories is anchored in gratitude compared to one living in negativity and self-criticism. A life of gratitude is celebrated as we slow down and love ourselves enough to enjoy the small moments of happiness in our day. In the same way we revel in our children's first words, foods, and steps, we can revel in wonder for our own life's small victories and firsts. Embrace your special moments, celebrate them, and let them propel you toward your larger aspirations. You deserve everything you seek: promotion, company, children, adventure, a healthy body—anything you dream up, you can achieve. Celebrate every step on your journey and love yourself deeper with a daily gratitude practice for what you have and where you're going!

"What comes to mind when I think of self-love is that every time family members, my ex, or his attorney dredge up my past alcohol addiction, I no longer feel shame or guilt. I am so proud that I got out of my own way in my own time, and six years later, I have an amazing story to tell other women who are lost in addiction trying to numb their pain. I tell them that they, too, can get out, repair and rebuild a bigger, better life. That's self-love for me."

Mona

Exercise: Reflect with Gratitude and Wonder on Your Victories

- Take a few moments to either close your eyes or open your journal and reflect on the small victories you've experienced today or this week. List them out.

- Revel in wonder and gratitude for them, celebrate them, and let them inspire you as you navigate your path to fulfillment and success. These small moments of triumph are not just steps along your path—they are the essence of growth and achievement and deserve your attention.

- Consider doing this daily to celebrate yourself and practice gratitude.

The Future of Self-Love: Evolving with Age and Wisdom

Aging is a part of the experience of life, something to be embraced. Yet, it is often framed within a narrative of decline and loss, especially for women. Society perpetuates the idea that aging is something to be feared or fought against, with countless products and services aimed at "defying" the natural aging process. However, this perspective overlooks the profound beauty and liberation that can accompany aging. Embracing the aging process as a rebellion against these societal norms allows for celebrating life's accumulated wisdom and experiences rather than mourning lost youth.

Many cultures worldwide celebrate a woman's aging and her transition into menopause. Tribes like the Maasai in Kenya and Tanzania celebrate menopause with ceremonies called "Emorata," where they celebrate the woman's transition into a new life stage where she can pass on knowledge to younger generations. In India, menopause is viewed as a time of freedom and sexuality and doesn't negatively affect her social standing. In Japan, menopause is called "konenki" and comprises three parts: energy, regeneration, and renewal. It's seen as a time of transition and a new purpose. Mayan and Cree cultures believe that women must enter menopause to access their shamanic and healing powers. In Native American cultures, post-menopausal women are considered "women of wisdom."

One of the most pervasive misconceptions about aging, particularly for women, is that it heralds a diminishing relevance and vibrancy. This stereotype is not only untrue, but also hurtful. Aging can be a time of growth and exploration. It is a phase marked by an accumulation of knowledge, self-awareness, and, often, a clearer sense of what truly matters in life. By challenging these negative stereotypes and shifting your focus to the positives of gaining experience and wisdom, you can foster a healthier, more empowering approach to aging.

Public figures who embrace their aging with grace and vitality can serve as powerful role models in this respect. Who are some you look up to? Many demonstrate that aging does not equate to a decline in creativity, passion, or influence but exemplifies strength and grace as they achieve, inspire, and contribute profoundly to their fields and society. Each phase of life holds tremendous potential if we only embrace it with positivity, resilience, and self-love.

Continuing self-care and maintaining physical health, mental sharpness, and emotional well-being as you age is important. This involves regular physical activity, keeping the mind active through reading, learning new skills, engaging in creative endeavors, and maintaining social connections with friends, family, and community. Skincare is also an essential part of our self-care as we age, as is caring for our hair and nails with the products and sunscreen that fit our needs. Facial massage and rejuvenation techniques, such as face yoga, lymph drainage, tapping, chi gong, gua sha, and many more, can be found on YouTube. Caring for your physical body will help you feel and look beautiful at any age. Regular checkups with health professionals should not be overlooked, as preventative care can significantly impact quality of life in later years.

As the seasons of life shift and turn, so does the nature of our self-love. With each passing year, the experiences we gather shape our existence and refine our understanding of self-love. Initially, your self-love practices are focused on building self-esteem or crafting a positive body image. However, these practices can evolve as you mature into more profound reflections on personal legacy, life satisfaction, and wisdom gained through diverse experiences. Embracing this dynamic approach ensures self-love adapts to meet your changing needs and circumstances, providing a stable foundation of care and respect for yourself at every stage of life.

Adapting your self-love practices as you age requires both introspection and flexibility. Begin by assessing your current practices and asking how they serve your needs today. You might find that activities that once filled you with joy no longer resonate as deeply. This shift is natural and expected. For instance, where vigorous physical exercise might have been a cornerstone of your self-love routine in earlier decades, you may now find more profound value in quieter, reflective practices such as meditation or journaling. Alternatively, social connections that once were nurtured through active engagement are better served through shared intellectual pursuits or meaningful conversations. Recognizing and embracing these shifts is not about diminishing your past practices but honoring your evolving needs.

Adapting your self-love practices as you age also involves integrating the wisdom gained from life's experiences. Wisdom is the deep knowledge from living through successes and setbacks, embracing joy, and navigating sorrow. It involves understanding that self-love is about not only self-care routines but also about making choices that align with your deepest values and aspirations. For example, forgiving past grievances, which once seemed impossible, becomes an essential practice of self-love, freeing you from old wounds and opening your heart to new joys. Similarly, wisdom might lead you to prioritize legacy-building activities, focusing on creating something enduring that reflects your values and contributions to the world.

As you age, your self-love practice can now include thinking about the future. Consider where you see yourself in the next decade or two. What aspects of your life do you wish to develop or preserve? Perhaps you aim to cultivate a rich garden of relationships filled with warmth and mutual support, or you aspire to contribute to your community in significant and lasting ways. By setting intentions for your future self, you engage in a proactive form of self-love that enhances your current well-being and sets the stage for continued growth and fulfillment. This forward-thinking approach ensures that your self-love practices evolve in ways that honor who you are and who you aspire to become.

When you recognize that each phase of life offers unique opportunities for learning, loving, and living fully, this acknowledgment enriches your journey and serves as a profound example to others around you. Self-love is a dynamic, enduring, and evolving force that adapts to embrace the complexities of life at every age. Self-love respects the maturity that comes with age and celebrates the ongoing journey of self-discovery and fulfillment.

Aging with self-love redefines your relationship to aging from one of fear to one of celebration. It recognizes and embraces the opportunities aging brings for continued growth and self-discovery. Aging with self-love is not about denying the changes that come with time but about celebrating the journey and embracing the wisdom that each year brings. It's about living with vibrancy and purpose, regardless of age, and challenging the stereotypes that society might impose on you. Aging then becomes an act of rebellion against societal expectations—a declaration that life's value does not diminish as the years pass but rather evolves into different forms of beauty and understanding. This shift is not only liberating and empowering but deeply enriching, offering a pathway to a fulfilling and vibrant life at any age.

"I was never taught anything about self-love when I was growing up. In fact, I learned those words in my 40s. It's not easy for me to receive money, compliments or presents. I'm learning more and more that self-love doesn't mean being narcissistic or egotistical but accepting the wonderful, changing, growing human being that I am (dark moments, good moments, and everything in between). I feel it's extremely important to teach self-love to the children, but we grown-ups need to learn first."

Alejandra

Exercise: What Will Your Legacy Be?

- Take some time to embrace how you are aging and consider your legacy. What do you want to leave the world with? How can you engage with the next generation to share your wisdom, stories, and skills?

- Consider documenting your life experiences in a journal or memoir as a legacy for future generations.

- Reflect on the rich tapestry of your life and this incredible journey you've been on with YOU. What an incredible ride. What a beautiful woman. Isn't she wonderful?

Conclusion

I want to acknowledge the remarkable journey of transformation you have embarked on with this handbook. From the initial steps of discovering self-love and embracing the nurturing practices of self-compassion and self-care, to the more advanced self-love techniques throughout our lifetime, you have shown incredible growth. This handbook aimed to be a compassionate and informative guide through the intricate landscape of self-love, and I am proud of your progress. The teachings on self-love and healing from the past, the vulnerable stories shared by women like you, and the practical and reflective exercises have undoubtedly begun to transform your relationship with yourself, building strength and resilience to carry you through your days. No matter what happens to you, your relationship with yourself is one constant that no one can take away from you!

Self-love is not a destination but a continuous journey. It is not merely a series of acts but an embodiment and a practice that enriches every facet of our existence. At the core of it is the fundamental belief that cultivating a compassionate and loving relationship with ourselves is the bedrock upon which we heal, grow, and forge meaningful connections with others. A life lived in self-love is a life worth living!

The journey of self-love is ongoing, a continuous process of learning to live with kindness and understanding toward ourselves. It requires patience, consistent practice, and a gentle acknowledgment of our human imperfections. I encourage you to revisit the strategies and insights shared in these pages often to deepen your practice and skills and continue nurturing your growth.

I also invite you to share the insights and transformations you experience with those around you. By fostering a community of support and understanding, we amplify the impact of our individual journeys and contribute to a culture where self-love and compassion are not just personal virtues but communal strengths. Why not start a book club where you can do the exercises together, talk about self-love, and learn from one another? You could even start a self-love meet-up via Zoom. I would also love it if you would share your journey by leaving a review online so that other women readers can receive the same benefits you did! We all deserve self-love.

As you move forward, let the principles of self-love guide your choices and interactions. Make decisions that honor your worth, create environments that support your well-being, and approach life's challenges with courage, self-respect, and self-compassion. You *will* mess up and feel disappointment, anger, sadness, and shame, but you can always share compassion with yourself in those painful or dark moments and return to self-love. Remember, every step taken in self-love is a step toward a more fulfilled and joyful life! You have the power to shape your life with self-love at its core.

Thank you sincerely for joining me on this journey. Your dedication to embracing the principles of self-love is a powerful testament to the beauty and strength inherent in each of us. May you continue to discover, with every passing day, deeper layers of joy, purpose, and fulfillment in your life. May your path be filled with gentle growth and boundless love, reminding you constantly of your worth and incredible capacity to shape a life of happiness and peace. Here's to a future where you stand firmly rooted in the essence of self-love, flourishing in all your endeavors and relationships.

Make a Difference with Your Review

Now that you have the handbook to practice and grow in self-love it's time to pass on your newfound knowledge and show other women where they can find the same.

Simply by leaving your honest opinion of this book on Amazon, you'll show other women just like you where they can find the self-love they're searching for.

Thank you for being on this self-love journey with me.

To make a difference, simply scan the QR code and leave a review:

Acknowledgments

I want to thank an exceptionally talented psychologist with a huge, compassionate heart, Dr. Aleksandra Kalinich, whom I am grateful to call a friend. Thank you for your guidance and insight as I prepared to share this work with others. Your insight, like your friendship, is such a gift. I also want to thank my first reader and supporter, Doreen Rice, and my editor, Beth Kujawski, who swooped in at the final hour and shared her enormous gifts. Finally, thank you to the Mikkelsen twins, who gave me the courage and tools to write again.

Recommended Reading

Boundaries:
Set Boundaries, Find Peace: A Guide to Reclaiming Yourself by Nedra Glover Tawwab
Boundaries Workbook by Nedra Glover Tawwab

Trauma:
Adult Children of Emotionally Immature Parents by Lindsay C. Gibson
The Body Keeps the Score by Bessel van der Kolk
Waking the Tiger by Peter Levine

Self-Compassion:
Self-Compassion by Kristin Neff
Fierce Self-Compassion by Kristin Neff
Radical Acceptance by Tara Brach

Forgiveness:
The Forgiveness Workbook: Cultivate Compassion, Release Resentment and Find Peace by Ilene S. Cohen

Friendship:

Modern Friendship by Anna Goldfarb

Intuitive Eating/Body Image:

Intuitive Eating by Evelyn Tribole & Elyse Resch

Gratitude:

The Little Book of Gratitude by Robert A. Emmons

Being a Woman:

Already Enough by Lisa Olivera

On Our Best Behavior by Elise Loehnen

Finances:

Worth It by Amanda Steinberg

References

- BetterUp. (n.d.). *Why vulnerability will change your life: The power of* .... https://www.betterup.com/blog/vulnerability
- Business Insider. (2015, July). *29 famous people who failed before they succeeded.* https://www.businessinsider.com/successful-people-who-failed-at-first-2015-7
- Calm. (n.d.). *7 advanced techniques to experience deep meditation.* https://www.calm.com/blog/deep-meditation
- California State University. (n.d.). *Creating critical media consumers.* https://www.calstate.edu/csu-system/news/Pages/media-literacy-critical-consumers.aspx
- Chopra. (n.d.). *The spiritual value of self-love.* https://chopra.com/blogs/personal-growth/the-spiritual-value-of-self-love
- Forté Foundation. (n.d.). *10 communication tips for women.* https://business360.fortefoundation.org/10-communication-tips-for-women/
- HelpGuide. (n.d.). *Imposter syndrome: Causes, types, and coping tips.* https://www.helpguide.org/articles/well-being-happiness/imposter-syndrome-causes-types-and-coping-tips.htm

- Hopkins Medicine. (n.d.). *Forgiveness: Your health depends on it.* https://www.hopkinsmedicine.org/health/wellness-and-prevention/forgiveness-your-health-depends-on-it
- Impossible Psych Services. (2023, November 15). *The impact of social media on self-esteem and body image.* https://www.impossiblepsychservices.com.sg/our-resources/articles/2023/11/15/the-impact-of-social-media-on-self-esteem-and-body-image
- Jones, M. (n.d.). *How parenting styles influence a child's self-esteem.* LinkedIn. https://www.linkedin.com/pulse/how-parenting-styles-influence-childs-self-esteem-michele-jones-ma
- Medical News Today. (n.d.). *Beauty standards and mental health: The connection and* https://www.medicalnewstoday.com/articles/beauty-standards-and-mental-health
- Nuffield Health. (n.d.). *How a digital detox can help you.* https://www.nuffieldhealth.com/article/how-a-digital-detox-can-help-you
- Northwestern Medicine. (n.d.). *Health benefits of having a routine.* https://www.nm.org/healthbeat/healthy-tips/health-benefits-of-having-a-routine#:~:text=An%20effective%20routine%20can%20help,emotional%20well%2Dbeing%20and%20energy
- PositivePsychology.com. (n.d.). *How to perform assertiveness training: 6 exercises.* https://positivepsychology.com/assertiveness-training/
- PositivePsychology.com. (n.d.). *Increase clients' self-love: 26 exercises & worksheets.* https://positivepsychology.com/self-love-exercises-worksheets/
- Psych Central. (n.d.). *Effects of emotional abuse on your brain, relationships,* https://psychcentral.com/health/effects-of-emotional-abuse

- Psych Central. (2020, April). *How to set boundaries with toxic people.* https://psychcentral.com/blog/imperfect/2020/04/how-to-set-boundaries-with-toxic-people
- Psych Central. (n.d.). *Emotional detox: 3 ways to cleanse yourself of stagnated emotions.* https://psychcentral.com/blog/emotional-detox-3-ways-to-cleanse-yourself-of-stagnated-emotions
- Psychology Today. (2019, June). *Self-love is the new #RelationshipGoals.* https://www.psychologytoday.com/us/blog/couples-thrive/201906/self-love-is-the-new-relationshipgoals
- Psychology Today. (2020, November). *Women and self-sabotage: How we sell ourselves short.* https://www.psychologytoday.com/us/blog/living-finesse/202011/women-and-self-sabotage-how-we-sell-ourselves-short
- Rifas, S. (n.d.). *Evolution of beauty: Across cultures and through the ages.* Medium. https://medium.com/@safirrifas34/evolution-of-beauty-across-cultures-and-through-the-ages-97d57a7ce41
- The Greater Good Science Center at UC Berkeley. (n.d.). *Evidence mounts that mindfulness breeds resilience.* https://greatergood.berkeley.edu/article/item/evidence_mounts_that_mindfulness_breeds_resilience
- The Greater Good Science Center at UC Berkeley. (n.d.). *How spending influences happiness.* https://greatergood.berkeley.edu/article/item/how_spending_influences_happiness
- U.S. National Library of Medicine, National Institutes of Health. (n.d.). *Editorial: Self-compassion: From neuroscience to clinical ...* https://www.ncbi.nlm.nih.gov/pmc/articles/PMC9358683/
- U.S. National Library of Medicine, National Institutes of Health. (n.d.). *Resilience after trauma: From surviving to thriving.* https://www.ncbi.nlm.nih.gov/pmc/articles/PMC4185140/

- U.S. National Library of Medicine, National Institutes of Health. (n.d.). *Self-affirmation activates brain systems associated with ...* https://www.ncbi.nlm.nih.gov/pmc/articles/PMC4814782/
- U.S. National Library of Medicine, National Institutes of Health. (n.d.). *Clinical EFT (emotional freedom techniques) improves ...* https://www.ncbi.nlm.nih.gov/pmc/articles/PMC6381429/
- U.S. National Library of Medicine, National Institutes of Health. (n.d.). *Ecotherapy – A forgotten ecosystem service: A review.* https://www.ncbi.nlm.nih.gov/pmc/articles/PMC6085576/
- U.S. National Library of Medicine, National Institutes of Health. (n.d.). *Online positive affect journaling in the improvement of ...* https://www.ncbi.nlm.nih.gov/pmc/articles/PMC6305886/
- U.S. National Library of Medicine, National Institutes of Health. (n.d.). *Social support and a sense of purpose: The role ...*https://www.ncbi.nlm.nih.gov/pmc/articles/PMC8793795/
- Harvard T.H. Chan School of Public Health. (n.d.). *Mindful eating - The nutrition source.* https://nutritionsource.hsph.harvard.edu/mindful-eating/
- Scientific American. (2016, June 6). *To stay sharp as you age, keep learning new skills.* Scientific American. Retrieved July 3, 2024, from https://www.scientificamerican.com/article/to-stay-sharp-as-you-age-learn-new-skills/
- Columbia University Mailman School of Public Health. (n.d.). *More schooling linked to slowed aging, increased longevity.* Columbia University Mailman School of Public Health News. Retrieved July 3, 2024, from https://www.publichealth.columbia.edu/news/more-schooling-linked-slowed-aging-increased-longevity#:~:text=Participants%20in%20the%20Framingham%20Heart,of%20Public%20Health%20and%20The

www.ingramcontent.com/pod-product-compliance
Lightning Source LLC
Chambersburg PA
CBHW070657130626
46553CB00005B/1746